THE SUMMIT

BOOK 3:
PURSUING GOD PASSIONATELY

JIM RAMOS

COPYRIGHT

DEDICATION

The Summit is dedicated to The Board. The years since The Great Hunt for God (now Men in the Arena) launched has been a life-changing journey of faith, trust, risk, and friendships. The Board consists of men from multiple states, denominations, and decades of life. These magnum men push and sharpen. They challenge and frustrate. They speak the truth without hesitation. They're more committed to The Great Hunt for God than to me—and that's how it should be. They are friends, brothers, and co-laborers in Christ. Each represents the apex of manhood in their passionate pursuit of Jesus. I respect them to no end.

These men, and their wives, champion The Great Hunt financially, pray continually, and invest countless hours pressing into our vision of transforming lives through teams of men. It's an indescribable honor to lock arms with them. Each brings his unique personality, skill set, and passion. I'm so blessed to journey with such upper echelon men.

TEAM CAPTAIN RESOURCES

You've received The Strong Men Series at a conference, from our website, your pastor, or possibly a friend. Now what? If you're holding this book, then you are a magnum enough man to figure it out on your own. This book is dangerous and has the power to change lives because within its pages are reference after reference from the Book of books.

You may still have some questions; we know this. We've provided several resources to help you on your journey to transform the lives of men and those they love, because when a man gets it—everyone wins.

First, check out our website (www.meninthearena.org). There you will find tons of great resources designed to inspire and equip you towards your best version.

Second, join thousands of men from around the world on our exciting Men in the Arena closed Facebook forum for men. Engage with men every day as they dialogue about what a man is and does. Do you need more help? We have a team of Arena Coaches ready to help you!

Third, subscribe to our wildly popular Men in the Arena Podcast. The Men in the Arena Podcast targets men living in the "Stress Bubble of Life" who are hardworking, loving one wife, raising godly children, and serving in their community.

Fourth, check out the QR Code before each meeting that links to an introductory video. Each video will help guide you to the best meeting possible.

SEND US A PICTURE OF YOUR TEAM

SEND US A PICTURE OF YOUR TEAM AND YOUR HERO STORY

We have no way of knowing who our resources are impacting, but we'd love to celebrate with you. Send us a picture of your team. We'll post it on social media and in our monthly newsletter if the photo is high quality and we have space.

Also, send us your stories of transformation that we call Hero Stories. God is the famous one, but He has chosen you to be the hero for your family. When a man gets it—everyone wins. If we happen to share your story, we will shoot you some swag to say, "Thanks!"

When you send the team picture, let us know where you're from (city, state, and/or country), who the leaders are, and where you meet (coffee shop, living room, church, etc.). Thank you for partnering with us.

INTRODUCTION

Sing to the Lord a new song, his praise from the ends of the earth, you who go down to the sea, and all that is in it, you islands, and all who live in them. Let the wilderness and its towns raise their voices; let the settlements where Kedar lives rejoice. Let the people of Sela sing for joy; let them shout from the mountaintops. Let them give glory to the Lord and proclaim his praise in the islands.
~ Isaiah 42:10-12

George Mallory was an English mountaineer who took part in the first three British expeditions to summit Mount Everest in the 1920's. Mallory died in 1924 attempting to summit the highest mountain in the world.

Among other things, he's remembered by his response to the question, "Why do you want to climb Mount Everest?"

He simply replied, "Because it's there." Why climb mountains?

For a man, the answer is as simple as Mallory's "because it's there." For some it may be for the challenge. For others still, it may be for the thrill of standing on the summit victorious—having defeated the mountain.

Men live for the challenge of the climb, to revel in the view from the top, to reap the rewards, and bragging rights of a greater conquest. An unspoken quest burning deep within a man is to find the hill that may take his life. Men long for a hill to die on—a signature mountain if you will. Men will search their entire lives for a mountain that defines them. At the worst it will kill them, at best it will be the legacy through which others remember them.

For the courageous few it's the summit or nothing, while the vast majority settle in the mundane valley of anonymity. The summit looms before our eyes. Are we open to its challenge? The mountain defining us is closer than you think. Abraham Lincoln once said, "Impossibilities vanish when a man and his God confront the mountain."

Confront the mountain. Accept the life-changing challenge. When it comes to understanding manhood—understand this— the pinnacle of manhood is radical devotion to Jesus Christ. In stereotypical stubbornness men still argue, "I've heard about Jesus, but I don't want to stop living my life."I translate their weak rebuttal as, "I'm happy being a male. I don't want to reach the apex of manhood. I don't want to be a complete man."

Jesus, the ultimate man, wants to lead you to the summit. Jesus is the same man who named his three best friends the Sons of Thunder and The Stone! He wants to make you a better man—the man you were created to be. To reject Jesus is to not only
accept eternity apart from God, but a lifetime of living in the lowlands.

How a man with the most basic understanding of God can't get this is beyond me. God made you (Psalm 139:1-18). God loves you. God has a mission for you. He lovingly crafted you while you were still in your mother's womb. How will you ever reach your potential as a man without extreme obedience to Him as your King?

You won't. It's impossible. You'll never be the man you were created for without reckless abandon to His Son, Jesus Christ. Is that clear enough? I hope so. Trust God completely. Let him be your guide up the treacherous trails of manhood. Let Him direct you to the top (Proverbs 3:5-6).

Isaiah understood this well, "Whether you turn to the right or to the left, your ears will hear a voice behind you, saying, 'This is the way; walk in it'" (Isaiah 30:21).

Do you want to conquer life—victorious? Do you want to reach the summit—a conqueror? Do you want to achieve the pinnacle of manhood? Give your life to Jesus. It's your only hope to summit the mountain of manhood.

A WORD FROM THE AUTHOR

Welcome to the multimedia edition of the Strong Men Study Series. In this new edition we've added QR codes at the beginning of each chapter. You can scan the QR codes with your smartphone or tablet to access all team meeting introductory videos. In these videos we introduce you to the content of each study. These brief presentations are designed to prepare your mind and heart for each team study.

At the end of the book you'll see a page called, "New Team Launch Steps" with QR codes leading up to your Men in the Arena team launch. The videos are a great resource for any man desiring to launch a new team. We emphatically recommend that every man partner with another man, to eventually start his own team. You've got this!

There are many QR readers available for smartphones and tablets. Check your device. It may already have one installed. Thank you so much for championing the cause of Christ on behalf of men because when a man gets it—everyone wins.

~ *Jim Ramos*

TABLE OF CONTENTS

TEAM MEETING ONE:
CUT IT STRAIGHT

We live in a time of spiritually passive men who can't see that we've become spiritual jellyfish flowing with cultural norms."
~ Bill Perkins

Welcome to The Summit!

The Summit is the third of five books in The Man Card Series. The Man Card refers to The Men in the Arena's definition of manhood: "protecting integrity, fighting apathy, pursuing God passionately, leading courageously and finishing strong."

Each of the five books in Strong Men Series contains ten great Bible studies along with fifty daily readings (five per week). The goal of each study is to inspire honest discussions. Studies are designed for the everyday guy and his pursuit of Jesus. They aren't designed for one man to lead, teach, or dominate discussions.

After each study are five daily readings from our "bathroom book for men", The Field Guide (see the ad in the back). Tackle one per day. Take notes. Meditate on it throughout the day. Come to each team meeting ready to discuss how you were challenged, encouraged, or had questions as you worked through the daily readings.

Give us your feedback (www.meninthearena.com). Let us know what you think.

Welcome to the Arena!

TEAM MEETING AT A GLANCE

- Opening Prayer, Weekly Announcements
- Personal and Victory Stories
- Each man will share his story — one man per week until all men have shared.
- After all men have shared their personal story, allow time each week for them to share victory stories.
- Weekly Study Closing Prayer
- Closing Prayer

> *"The goal of every man should be to know the Word better than anyone in his family."*
> ~ Men in the Arena

Share your thoughts on the statement, "*When a man gets it—everyone wins.*"

All throughout Scripture, God starts with men. Look at these examples:

- The human race started with a man—Adam.
- The covenant of the testaments was given to a man—Abraham.
- The twelve tribes of the nation Israel began with a man—Jacob (Israel).
- The redemption of Israel was given through a man—Moses.
- The occupation of the Promised Land was led by a man—Joshua.
- The royal prototype of the Messiah was a man—David.
- The Savior of the World came as a man—Jesus.
- Jesus began his ministry with twelve men—The Disciples.
- The leader of the first church was a man—Peter.
- The apostle bringing the gospel to the Gentile world was a man—Paul.
- The spiritual leader of your family is a man—You.

Were these men perfect? What did God use to shape their faith? You also might want to compare to others listed in the Faith Hall of Fame.
Hebrews 11:1-14

What does faith—trusting God—look like in the real world?
Psalm 42:1-2, Proverbs 3:5-6, Matthew 6:28-34, Philippians 3:12-14, and Jeremiah 29:13

What if a multi-tool was invented that offered a 100% money-back guarantee that if you read and followed the instructions, your life would be changed forever? What if it not only carried a lifetime guarantee but a generational guarantee?

You could pass it down through your lineage and it would guarantee life change for all who read and obeyed its instruction manual. This tool transcends the longest of times, the latest of technologies, and the harshest of treatments? Would you be in? Would you want to do whatever it tells you to?

The only reliable measuring tool confirming the Spirit's voice, the truth in a sermon, a word "from God", the advice from a Christian brother, or God's will for you—is the Bible!

How do you know that your faith is true, straight, and accurate? How do you know when your faith becomes crooked?
2 Timothy 2:14-19

In 2 Timothy 2:15 Paul warns Timothy to "correctly handle(s) the word of truth." He uses the Greek word orthotomeo for "correctly handle," which is translated as "cut it straight" like a craftsman cutting a straight line, a mason setting a straight line of bricks, a farmer plowing a straight furrow, or a worker building a straight road.

How does God use the Bible to cut it (your life) straight? How does God direct your path?
Hebrews 4:12-13

What other insights can you gain about the reliability of the Bible?
Psalm 119:9-11, 2 Timothy 3:14-17, and 2 Peter 1:20-21

Go back to 2 Timothy 3:16-17. What four elements does the Word of God help a man cut? Where does God use his Word in our lives?

All Scripture is God-breathed and is useful for teaching, rebuking, correcting, and training in righteousness, so that the man of God may be thoroughly equipped for every good work.

Where is "teaching" required for men? Who do men teach? Who do you lead? Where do you contribute to others?

Men are mandated to wash their wives with the Word of God in Ephesians 5:25-26. Therefore, we should know it better than anyone else in our household.

What does "rebuking" cut through? Who needs you to reach out to them? How can you use their incorrect statements and philosophies to win them to Christ? Whose lies do you need to cut through?

"When we rebuke—*elegmos*—someone's incorrect statements about God and life, we cut through the lies and bring them closer to the truth. Rebuking according to God's Word is one of the four greatest sources of evangelism."

"The Greek word for rebuking is elegmos. This is the only occurrence in the New Testament. Elegmos is used for conviction of a sinner."
~ Expositor's Bible Commentary

Faith is a narrow road. God uses guardrails found in the Bible to get us back on course. How does God use "correcting" to cut a straight line of faith? Where have you veered off course?

The Greek word for correcting is *epanorthosin*. This is the only place this word is found in the New Testament.

God turns males into men by training them in the Word of God. What does "training in righteousness" mean? Righteousness can be explained as "right ways." Share about a time God used the Bible to point you down the right way.

"Training, paideia, comes from pais, or child. It originally meant, 'the training of a child.'"
~ Expositor's Bible Commentary

"Epanorthosin means 'Restoration to an upright position or state.'"
~ Expositor's Bible Commentary

For you Star Wars fans, Paideia sure sounds a lot like the term for Jedi knights in training—Padwan.

Break into groups of three or four.

What area can you grow in becoming a man of the Word?

Take a moment today and share an encouraging Bible verse with the man next to you.

STUDY NOTES

_____

_____

_____

_____

_____

_____

_____

_____

_____

_____

_____

_____

_____

For the next five days, read the following entries from our **The Field Guide: A Bathroom Book for Men.**

We hope they challenge and encourage you to get in the great Arena for God. See you on the Arena Floor!

MAN FULLY ALIVE

The glory of God is man fully alive.
~ St. Irenaeus

I sat next to the fireplace at a coffee house reflecting on life when I noticed the cup in my hand. Written across the bottom was a quote. Like the Bible verses on the bottom of In-N-Out Burger soda cups—there it was. A quote from a man I'd never heard of named Irenaeus. Written around 185 AD, his words changed my life: "The glory of God is man fully alive."

They hit me like a punch below the belt—especially when compared to my life verse—John 10:10, "The thief comes only to steal and kill and destroy; I have come that they may have life, and have it to the full."

I'd become fat and satisfied with living in a rut. Was this life to the fullest?

Was this what being fully alive for Christ looked like? I'd become a partially alive eggshell of a man. But I wanted to live. And I wanted life now.

Coffee in hand, I chose life and all the risks that living with abandon brings. I chose to be fully alive and fully glorify the God who breathed His life into me. I decided to move forward every day.

I decided to laugh more, love more, and live more. I vowed to love Shanna and my sons to the best of my ability. I resolved that when failure knocks me down (and it will) I'll get back up, shake the dust off, and start tomorrow new, fresh, and alive.

I want my one life to be enough. I want my one life to matter. I want it to count for God.

A month later, we launched The Great Hunt for God.

HIDE AND SEEK GOD

God does not hide things from His children.
He hides them for His children.
~ Bill Johnson

Men need challenges to keep them fully alive. As an adult it's been sports, fitness, and the outdoors. For me, hunting is more than simply killing. It's an experience on the soul level. The wilderness beckons me to journey deeper with nothing but my gear and camp on my back.

As the summer starts to fade—the days grow short, and the air becomes crisp—I hear the whisper in the wind of the wilderness calling me. It compels me to explore further, journey deeper, and climb higher.

My soul longs to journey into the mountains to meet my Creator. It's in the mountains where I sense God's silent call, His sovereign pleasure, and supreme freedom.

But one mistake in the wilderness could mean certain death. Thus, I prepare for whatever weather heaven throws my way. The wilderness calls. But it never begs. I can take it or leave it. The choice is always mine. Our great hunt is no different. God isn't needy or desperate.

He beckons, but never begs. He calls us but doesn't need us. He speaks but doesn't shout. Men fail to hear Him not because He isn't speaking but because they refuse to pursue Him. God knows men need to be challenged to seek the God who is not easy to find. Jeremiah 29:13 beckons us forward, "You will seek me and find me when you seek me with all your heart."

The challenge is to hunt, stalk, to pursue God.

"Seek first his kingdom"
Matthew 6:33

Develop the eyes of a hunter. Look for God in the small things. God is not hiding from us. He's hiding for us. Those who pursue the hard-to-find Creator of the Universe will find Him.

Stay in the game.

EVER INCREASING CAPACITY

Leaders should ask themselves, is my heart for God increasing?
Is my capacity for loving God deepening?
~ Bill Hybels

I'm ashamed at our generation's dishonor toward our elders—especially in our churches. Tradition isn't necessarily religion. Music styles don't represent spiritual depth. Who will reject the multi-generational church models that separate age groups?

Who will lock arms with all ages through an intergenerational ministry approach? Who will build bridges between generations instead of burning them?

Will we demand the same respect we haven't given to those who've gone before us from the generations that follow?

We don't have all the answers to life's many questions, but those who've gone before us are a great resource for wisdom needed to navigate life.

In 1 John 2:12-14 a spiritual distinction is made between "little children" (spiritually immature), "young men" (spiritually sound but lacking experience), and "fathers" (seasoned men of God).

Understanding the distinction between spiritual maturity and chronological age; The Great Hunt is an intergenerational movement targeting men from all decades of life. For example, the spiritual "fathers" of our group have wisdom to offer the "young men."

Young men, in turn, bring their vision and passion, while the "little children" ignite us with their ignorant enthusiasm.

Ask yourself, "Am I increasing my capacity to love God, love people, and hatred toward sin?" If a man is not different in five years than he is today, he's in danger of falling into a religious pit of traditionalism instead of a dynamic faith that's ever expanding.

Maybe this is exactly what the Apostle Paul was thinking when he penned, "I am confident of this very thing; that He who began a good work in you will carry it on to completion" (Philippians 1:6).

DRIVING TOO SLOW

As Saul turned to leave Samuel, God changed Saul's heart,
and all these signs were fulfilled that day.
~ 1 Samuel 10:9

A pastor told me about an event he witnessed between two children. He found them fighting and separated them: "When I come back I want to see that your angry eyes have changed." But when he returned one boy had his middle finger raised toward the other boy in an obvious act of aggression.

The pastor asked, "Do you know what you are doing?"
"Yes," responded the boy as he stared, finger in the air, at the wide-eyed boy across the room.
"Tell me what that middle finger means?"
Still staring angrily, the boy said, "It means you're driving too slow!"

Obviously he hadn't experienced a change of heart. I wonder where he learned what that middle finger meant! The pastor knew a great secret. When the heart changes the eyes change.

When the eyes change, the actions change. Maybe this is why Paul prays in Ephesians 1:18, "that the eyes of your heart may be enlightened."

Experience teaches us to change our behavior, but only God can change the heart. This is what separates Christianity from other religions. It's a relationship with God that changes a man from the inside out. Religion attempts to change a man from the outside in.

But the way to change your family tree is with a change of heart that only comes through radical devotion to Jesus.

Religious behaviors don't impress God. He desires a heart fully devoted to Him.

What is God saying to your heart? What is He teaching you? How are you changing because of what He is doing in you?

HEART AND SOUL

"Do all that you have in mind," his armor-bearer said. "Go ahead; I am with you heart and soul."
~ 1 Samuel 14:7

I once coached a high school football team that highlighted a "no huddle" offense. We utilized code words for formations, strong versus weak sides, and pass protection. The same run play had a name designating strong side and another for the weak.

For example, "Heart" was our strong side counter play, and "Soul" was the same play to the weak side.

Although distinctly different, the heart and soul are often used in tandem.

The heart is our core. It's the essence of who we are. It's the inner, true self (Matthew 12:34-36). In other words, the heart is "who you are."

Your heart, however, is directly influenced by the soul.

The soul has authority over the heart. The soul has the power to choose beyond the primal needs for survival. It has the ability to determine one's destiny. The soul is what God referred to when He said, "Let's make man in our image," (Genesis 1:26). It separates man from every other living thing.

Vine's Expository Dictionary defines the soul as the, "immaterial, invisible part of a man; the seat of will and purpose, the seat of appetite, the invisible man, the seat of new life."

If the heart is "who you are", the soul is "what you are." It's your naked self, "laid bare" (Hebrews 4:13) before God.

Can you say to God, "I am with you heart and soul" (1 Samuel 14:7)?

Does God have all of who you are as well as all of what you are?

Does He have your heart and your soul?

TEAM MEETING TWO: WALKING

> *"We need dangerous men in the church...It's a sure sign of church health when dangerous men start showing up on Sunday. But they won't stay unless we stop condemning them and learn to speak their language: the language of risk."*
> ~ David Murrow, Why Men Hate Going to Church

What did you take away from last week's study and daily readings? What are you still processing? What challenged your current paradigm? What inspired you to grow as a man?

What measuring rod do you use when someone tells you they are a "Christian"? How do you know if someone is the real deal when it comes to walking with God? Why is it important to discern the statement, "I'm a Christian"?

Matthew 7:1 may be the most violated verse in the Bible where Jesus warns that if we judge, then we'll be judged. Then, just a few verses down (16) he advises that we will know his true followers by the fruit they bear. We must resolve the tension between discerning and judging—but in no way are we to turn a blind eye to false witnesses and fruitless lives.

How do you measure the health of your relationship with God and the mission He has for you? When do you know you've veered off course? How do you determine sin in your life?

Faith in Jesus is more of a process than an event. It's about walking by faith more than taking a leap of faith.

TEAM MEETING AT A GLANCE

- Opening Prayer, Weekly Announcements
- Personal and Victory Stories
- Each man will share his story — one man per week until all men have shared.
- After all men have shared their personal story, allow time each week for them to share victory stories.
- Weekly Study Closing Prayer
- Closing Prayer

> *"I have been driven many times upon my knees by the overwhelming conviction that I had nowhere else to go."*
> ~ Abraham Lincoln

Check out Enoch's epitaph in Genesis 5:24. What do you think about this?

Enoch walked with God; then he was no more, because God took him away.

Enoch is also mentioned in the Hebrews 11:5-6 Faith Hall of Fame.

> *By faith Enoch was taken from this life, so that he did not experience death: 'He could not be found, because God had taken him away.' For before he was taken, he was commended as one who pleased God. And without faith it is impossible to please God, because anyone who comes to him must believe that he exists and that he rewards those who earnestly seek him.*

What does it look like to "walk by faith, not by sight"?
2 Corinthians 5:7 (NASB)

Men in the Arena uses the acrostic W.A.L.K.I.N.G. with God as a great tool to measure (not judge) your faith, and the faith of others. Note the progressive tense of the verb. Walking by faith is a process more than an event.

Worshiping. How is worship more than music? How is music a great worship tool? What do the following verses teach us about "worshipping God"?
Psalm 86:9, 95:6, 99:5, 100:2, and John 4:20-24

Worship is more than music. *Proskuneo* is one of the many words used in the Bible for worship. It appears in the New Testament fifty-nine times (nine times in John 4), which is more times than all ten other words for worship combined!

Proskuneo means to fawn or crouch—to prostrate oneself in homage. It literally means to kiss, like a dog licking his master's hand.

Approaching God in scheduled blocks of prayer. Men are compartmental, focused, task-oriented beings. Schedule a time of prayer like so many in scripture. Look at the men who had specific moments of prayer as they walked with God.
Matthew 6:9-13,14:23, Acts 10:9, and 1 Thessalonians 5:17

"Excusing away a weak prayer life by quoting a verse out of context: 'I pray without ceasing' (1 Thessalonians 5:17) is ridiculous."

With two ears and one mouth you should spend twice as much time listening for God than speaking to Him.

Loving other Christians through fellowship. What can you learn from the following verses about locking arms with other believers? What value do others offer to our faith?
Matthew 12:30, Hebrews 10:24-25, and John 13:34-35

Experience teaches that fellowship is one of the first things to go when our walk with God is challenged or backslides.

Knowing the Word of God (review last week's study). Here are some of last week's review verses about the value of the Word of God.
Psalm 119:9-10, 2 Timothy 3:16-17, Hebrews 4:12, and 2 Peter 1:20-21

Investing your resources in the Kingdom of God. Everything you have is yours on loan, so hold on loosely. What do the following verses teach us about our resources?
Matthew 25:14-29, Acts 2:42-45, Romans 13:8, 2 Corinthians 8:2-5, and 9:7

> *"Every Christian is a minister and every minister has a ministry."*
> ~ David Grinder

How tightly you hold onto the things God has asked you to steward says a lot about your faith. Look at items you may have with you now: your keys represent your possessions, wristwatch represents your time, wedding ring represents your marriage, phone represents your relationships, and your wallet represents money.

Nurturing others into disciples. Who are you nurturing on their spiritual journey as a follower of Jesus? Who are you praying for? Who are you reaching out to?
Matthew 28:19-20.

The Bible teaches the Church to make disciples of Christ not decisions for Christ. Giving your life away in Christian service. Look at the following verses that talk about the importance of serving God according to your gifts.
Romans 12:3-8, 1 Corinthians 12:12-30, Ephesians 2:8-10, 4:10-16, 2 Timothy 4:6-8, James 1:21-23, and 2:18-26.

BONUS MATERIAL

There is not enough time in this meeting to study all of this material. Take the time this week to study this section. As a leader you may wish to make it a stand-alone meeting.
Go for it!

What is your S.H.A.P.E.
What are your Spiritual gifts? What unique gifts has God given you subsequent to your salvation?
1 Corinthians 12:1-30, 14:1-39, Romans 12:6-8, and Ephesians 4:11-13

What breaks your Heart? What hill will you die on? What are you passionate about? What wrecks you?
Luke 17:7-10, 24:32, Acts 9:15, and Philippians 3:13,

Every man should ask God to give him a "Popeye Moment" where he passionately declares, "That's all I can stand. I can't stand no more!"

What Abilities, talents, and skills have you learned? What are you naturally good at?
Exodus 35:30-36:2, Psalm 139:14-16, Matthew 25:15-28, and Acts 11:27-29

Which is your basic Personality? Do people energize you or suck the life out of you? Are you an introvert or extrovert? Do you paint the world with small brush strokes or large? Generally speaking, what is your temperament?
Corinthians 12:23-26

There are a myriad of personality profile tests out there. Google them and take one! We love Florence Litaver's Personality Plus.

The S.H.A.P.E. concept was first taught by Rick Warren in his classic book The Purpose Driven Church.

What Experiences has life thrown your way? What hand has life dealt? How have your choices affected you? What traumatic life experiences do you bring to the table? What great experiences have you had? Where have you experienced healing?
Romans 5:3-5, 8:28, James 1:2-4, and 2 Corinthians 12:9-10

Break into groups of three or four.

Where can you grow in WALKING with God?

Take a moment today and pray for each other.

STUDY NOTES

_____

_____

_____

_____

_____

_____

_____

_____

_____

_____

_____

_____

For the next five days, read the following entries from our **The Field Guide: A Bathroom Book for Men.**

We hope they challenge and encourage you to get in the great Arena for God. See you on the Arena Floor!

WALKING IN CIRCLES

To whom will you run for help? Where will you leave your riches?
~ Isaiah 10:3

One of my favorite features on a GPS (Global Positioning System) is the Plotter feature, which enables you to follow your own footsteps. This is useful feature, especially when navigating in the dark. But I'll never trust my life to an electronic device. I carry a compass for backup.

My friend Justin trusted a GPS to guide him while packing a bull elk to his rig during a snowstorm. After an hour of walking in the darkness, he crossed over some familiar tracks—his! He'd been walking in circles because the GPS couldn't receive a clear satellite signal during the blizzard.

His story teaches a valuable lesson. Trust only in what will never fail.

Isaiah 10:3 asks, "Where will you leave your riches?"

A man may spend years running at success, but his pursuits will eventually malfunction. If he's fortunate, his wealth will carry him to the end of life where he'll face judgment, only to realize that he who dies with the most toys— still dies
(Hebrews 9:27).

A great rule to live by is, "But seek first his kingdom and his righteousness, and all these things will be given to you as well" (Matthew 6:33).

What matters most isn't how much success you achieve, but how you can glorify your God.
1 Timothy 6:17 says, "Command those who are rich in this present world not to be arrogant nor to put their hope in wealth, which is so uncertain, but to put their hope in God, who richly provides us with everything for our enjoyment."

Decide to make Christ your ultimate pursuit. Run towards His riches. He'll never disappoint you. And He will never send you walking in circles.

BLEEDING HEARTS

The Lord your God will circumcise your hearts and the hearts of your descendants, so that you may love him with all your heart and with all your soul, and live.
~ Deuteronomy 30:6

Once, while shopping, I ran into a woman from church who introduced herself and her son. He proudly pulled up his shirt to expose a scar that ran from his chest to his stomach and said, "I had heart surgery! Do you have any scars?"

Not to be outdone by a five-year-old I showed him the twelve-inch scar on my left knee, three-inch scar on my side, two-inch scar on my hand, smaller cuts from a mountain bike accident, and a shower-fall scar under my chin.

I joked about the scar over my heart from the high school sweetheart who broke it. He didn't get it. But nothing could compete with the scar of this five-year- old boy.

His scars got me thinking. Scars have three things in common: they're a reminder of healing, they were once open wounds cleansed by blood, and they remind us of a time of pain in life. Scars represent pain, purification, healing. Blood a cleansing agent as well as a symbol of covenant.

We see this on the female body. Women are equipped with a patch of skin around the vaginal opening that serves no biological purpose—except covenant.

Blood is produced after first intercourse when the Hymen is broken. Physically insignificant, the Hymen is a sign of a spiritual covenant (Jeremiah 34:18) between a man, woman, and God.

Circumcision is another sign of the covenant made obsolete by the covenant blood of Jesus (Acts 15:9).

Heart circumcision, however, doesn't come easy and often results from a catastrophic event God uses to cut through a heart calloused by sin. Has your heart bled as a symbol of your commitment to God?

UPGRADES

What good will it be for a man if he gains the whole world, yet forfeits his soul?
Or what can a man give in exchange for his soul?
~ Matthew 16:26

We live in a world of upgrades. In 1991, I bought a beautiful mountain bike and maintained it by only buying upgrades to replace broken components. Twenty years later I still have that bike and the only original components are the bar ends.

A fisherman's home is littered with tackle upgrades. A hunter's garage is filled with camouflage upgrades. The golfer's shed is filled with old clubs. Visit a man's yard sale and you'll see his old upgrades.

The same can be said for motor heads, computer geeks, and sports fanatics. We love to upgrade, but there is one thing we must never attempt to trade up for—our soul.

We can all think of one man—maybe many—who appeared to have it all: an amazing career, beautiful wife, successful children, all the toys, and a huge home to store it all. He once thrived as a Christian, serving the Lord in dynamic fashion, but got rich and traded it all in for pleasure. He surrendered his soul for stuff, wrongly believing it was an upgrade.

Don't be that man.

A man's treasure is not found in the accumulation of stuff, but a heart committed to the King. The world and its stuff won't pass into eternity, but the work done for Jesus continues. Be careful not to waste your life in pursuit of the world's fading treasures (2 Corinthians 4:18). Relationships crossover. Resources don't.

And remember, "For where your treasure is, there your heart will be also" (Matthew 6:21).

YOUR MESSAGE

Even as he was speaking, Jonathan son of Abiathar the priest arrived.
Adonijah said, "Come in. A worthy man like you must be bringing good news."
~ 1 Kings 1:42

When I was a senior in high school, I attended our Senior Awards Night where classmates were awarded according to their achievements. Every student—all 200 of them—would receive some creatively titled award. Since two of my best friends were in charge of the awards, I was excited to hear mine.

When my time came, I heard the words that would haunt me, "Jim Ramos, is awarded the most likely to be on the cover of Sports Illustrated."

I stood up, pumped up my chest, and proudly began to strut to the platform. As I reached it my two "friends" smiled and continued in unison, "...and tell you about it!"

That embarrassing moment taught me a life lesson. We all communicate a message to the world.

What's yours?

It appears from scripture that men, like Jonathan son of Abiathar, were sent as messengers based on character qualities. A good man meant good news; a bad man meant bad news. This way a leader could identify the news before it arrived. This could explain why Adonijah was shocked when Jonathan son of Abiathar brought bad news instead.

The word gospel means nothing more than "good news." The message of Jesus is a message of salvation and life. It's great news. When men see you coming, what do they anticipate your message will be?

Do you represent the good news of Jesus? Or, do you communicate some lesser representation of who Jesus is?

Every man brings a message. Know yours. And communicate it consistently.

POWER

A wise man has great power, and a man of knowledge increases strength...
~ Proverbs 24:5

I once heard a gray-haired preacher define power as, "The supernatural ability to get things done." I had to agree. Power is the supernatural ability to accomplish the miraculous: the forming of a human life, the salvation of a soul, or the physical healing of the sick.

But in the American workweek jungle, men often need a miracle to accomplish their daily tasks. Oftentimes I walk into the office with my game face on, uncertain of whether I'll finish a message, complete a study, or find a much-needed volunteer.

Yet, there are many days when I end the day amazed at what God did. It's such a blessing knowing that tasks were miraculously completed thanks to the power of God (Ephesians 3:20-21).

Power is the supernatural ability to get things done. We need the power of God. A good man can protect his integrity, fight apathy, lead courageously, and finish strong. But he's an incomplete man if not passionately pursuing the God who created him.

Without Christ in his life, he's only a partial man.

The pinnacle of power is released when a man passionately pursues God. Power is a byproduct of a life permeated by Jesus. Jesus is the source of power. He's the only source.

If a man wants true power in his life he must relinquish all his control to the power of the Holy Spirit through Jesus Christ.

TEAM MEETING THREE: GODHUNTERS

> *"The ordinary man is passive…against major events, he is as helpless as against the elements. So far from endeavoring to influence the future, he simply lies down and lets things happen to him."*
> ~ George Orwell

What did you take away from last week's study and daily readings? What are you still processing? What challenged your current paradigm? What inspired you to grow as a man?

When talking about a defining Bible chapter for women, Proverbs 31 usually comes up. Men, consider Job 29 as the defining chapter for us.

Job 29 is titled "Job's Final Defense" as he reflects on life prior to the tragedies that struck him. Here is an excerpt from Job 29:2-4.

> *How I long for the months gone by, for the days when God watched over me, when his lamp shone upon my head and by his light I walked through darkness! Oh, for the days when I was in my prime, when God's intimate friendship blessed my house.*
> ~ Job 29:2-4

Which of the above lines stands out to you? How would you explain it? What can you gather about Job's relationship with God from the above passage? As a group, think of a verse to support your answers.
Example: "By his light I walked through darkness." Support Verse: Psalm 119:105, "Your word is a lamp for my feet, a light on my path."

What did God have to say about His relationship with Job? What would God say about His relationship with you?
Job 1:1-8

TEAM MEETING AT A GLANCE

- Opening Prayer, Weekly Announcements
- Personal and Victory Stories
- Each man will share his story — one man per week until all men have shared.
- After all men have shared their personal story, allow time each week for them to share victory stories.
- Weekly Study Closing Prayer
- Closing Prayer

> *"We can say with confidence that we have never known a man whose life has changed in any significant way apart from regular study of God's Word."*
> ~ Patrick Morely, No Man Left Behind

The goal of every man should be to pursue God, know the Word, serve others, and trust Him with more abandon than anyone in his family.

The word Godhunter was created to describe a man's relationship to God. It originates from Philippians 3:12-14 where Paul—two times—uses the phrase "press on." Where can you "press on" in your relationship with God? Where have you hit the pause button in your God pursuit?

The Greek word *dioko* means "I pursue." It is translated in Philippians 3:12 and 14 as "press on." *Dioko* was a word used in hunting as well as track and field meaning "I pursue." It is a strong expression for active and relentless pursuit.

Translate Paul's words "I press on" in Philippians 3:12 and 14. Put these verses in your own words.

God is man's ultimate trophy and only worthy pursuit. What do you discover when you compare Philippians 3:7-10 (specifically 8) with 3:12-14 (specifically 13)? Do you see anything interesting or noteworthy?

> *"The impulse to pursue God originates with God, but the outworking of that impulse is our following hard after Him."*
> ~ A.W. Tozer, The Pursuit of God

Skubala is the Greek word for dung or rubbish in Philippians 3:8. In common language it was used to mean that which is thrown to the dogs. In medical language it means excrement or dung. Paul had to let go of the crap in his life in order to pursue the real prize.

Review last week's meeting. What does it mean to "know Christ?" Do you know Christ? Better yet, does Christ know you? Explain. Matthew 7:21-23

God isn't interested in you knowing trivial facts about Him. He wants to know you personally. More than that, is for you to know Him personally.

Go back to Job 29:1-6. Job had an "intimate friendship" (verse 4) with God. What does that look like in your life?

Ginosko—properly to know, especially through personal experience (first-hand acquaintance)."
~ HELPS Word Studies

> *"You say that you know God, but the better question is: does God know you?"*
> ~ Anonymous

Break into groups of three or four.

What can you do to know Christ more?

Take a moment today and pray for each other.

> *"If knowing Christ is experiencing him through a personal relationship, then what does that look like for a man of God?"*
> ~ Kenneth S. Wuest,
> Word Studies in the Greek New Testament

STUDY NOTES

_____

_____

_____

_____

_____

_____

_____

_____

_____

_____

_____

_____

For the next five days, read the following entries from our **The Field Guide: A Bathroom Book for Men.**

We hope they challenge and encourage you to get in the great Arena for God. See you on the Arena Floor!

MAN OF PRAYER

In return for my friendship they accuse me, but I am a man of prayer.
~ Psalm 109:4

The man who believes in gods other than Jesus can still model manly traits, lead his family well, serve in his community, and even attend church. I know ungodly men who are, in many ways, examples of manhood.

To say a man can't be a good man without Christ is naive and incorrect.

The problem is that manhood without Jesus at the center is a shell. The best a good man will ever be can't compare to that same man committed to Jesus. Jesus makes him more of a man—a whole man.

Jesus is the pinnacle of manhood. No man is a total man apart from Jesus Christ. There are certain qualities that bring depth to a man. One of these is prayer. Paul admonished the men of Thessalonica to, "pray without ceasing" (1 Thessalonians 5:17 NASB).

Jesus taught his followers how to pray (Matthew 6:9-14). There's more to manhood than meets the eye. Underneath the surface of manhood is a life of prayer. Prayer stands a man before the Creator daily, begging for blessings over his family members, friends, and community.

I once heard a speaker compare men to waffles; compartmentalized. Women, he explained, are interconnected like spaghetti. Men being compartmentalized tend to focus on one task at a time, while women are partially engaged in many tasks at once.

Start by compartmentalizing your day with prayer. Set a time to zero in on prayer.

Immerse yourself in the presence of God.

Put God on your calendar of every-day events. Then you'll understand what it means to be a complete man.

BEEF WITH COMMUNION

Therefore, whoever eats the bread or drinks the cup of the Lord in an unworthy manner will be guilty of sinning against the body and blood of the Lord. A man ought to examine himself before he eats of the bread and drinks of the cup.
~ 1 Corinthians 11:27-28

I have a personal beef with how churches participate in communion. My beef began two decades ago at a youth camp on Catalina Island's Camp Fox. The camp traditionally ended on Easter Sunday with a sunrise service for the two hundred high school campers.

The service concluded with a strong message with a warning, "Communion is only for believers and if you are not a follower of Jesus do not take communion—or else!"

Or else what, I wondered? They might be condemned to an eternity in hell? That's already happening. That can't be it. But what's worse than hell?

Then I figured out why I had a beef with communion. Maybe the focus should be on those who call themselves "Christians", but aren't walking in obedience, rather than the unsaved. Let's focus on the men who aren't giving or serving in their churches, but partake in communion as if nothing is wrong.Paul did.

Communion is a time of reflection and examination. Am I living in obedience to Jesus? Am I faithful in giving? Do I serve others in Jesus' name? Do I have a conflict with any other person in my life? Am I hiding sin?

Communion without examination is judgment. The man of God lives between the lines of loving God and testing his life. We are told to "Test yourselves to see if you are in the faith" (2 Corinthians 13:5-NASB).

Why are so many men sick, weak, or asleep in the Church today? Maybe we need to focus communion on what really matters, the lost souls within the Church who don't realize how lost they really are.

CURSING AND BLESSINGS

When Balak son of Zippor, the king of Moab, prepared to fight against Israel, he sent for Balaam son of Beor to put a curse on you. But I would not listen to Balaam, so he blessed you again and again, and I delivered you out of his hand.
~ Joshua 24:9-10

In the early 1990's a pastor warned me of a satanic cult praying curses upon the Campus Life club I directed. He admonished me to fight back in prayer.

I took his advice.

What followed was fourteen years of life-changing ministry in that community. But I learned how vital prayer is to any work of God.

In our brief time leading The Great Hunt, we've recruited nearly one thousand Prayer Force members. They go to battle for men and beg for God's favor over this fledgling movement. It's a war the enemy knows he'll lose, but will continue to fight nonetheless.

You see, Satan wants to curse what God is blessing. The goal is to seek God's blessing in everything.

Rick Warren once said, "I never curse what God is blessing." This is wise advice. Balak son of Zipper, the king of Moab, knew he couldn't beat Israel, so he sent for Balaam to curse them. When Balaam realized they were a blessed people he refused to curse them, essentially saying, "If you can't beat 'em, join them!"

You can't curse what God is blessing. You won't defeat that which God has proclaimed victorious.

Men who follow Jesus have won the war and received the blessing of salvation (Ephesians 2:8-10). Still, we must fight onward to remain in God's blessing.

FOUR - ONE - THREE

I know what it is to be in need, and I know what it is to have plenty. I have learned the secret of being content in any and every situation, whether well fed or hungry, whether living in plenty or in want. I can do everything through him who gives me strength.
~ Philippians 4:12-13

The man who led me to Christ has a son who played college baseball as a pitcher. He wrote 4-1-3 on the top of his spikes as a motivator while he was in his wind up. It stands for Philippians 4:13. His Dad often yelled, "4-1-3" as he wound up to pitch, reminding him that the numbers on the top of his spikes represented who he was playing for.

As we study Philippians 4:12, we see that Paul's reliance upon Christ for strength resulted in contentment. He'd learned the secret of contentment by hitting life's curve balls. In the midst of pain, hunger, and persecution Paul learned that Jesus offered strength to those who trusted Him.

Often, the strength God gives isn't the strength to win or prosper but to endure and persevere. Winning is a means to the end of developing the habit of trusting God completely.

The balance however, is learning to trust God with our gifts and abilities without letting them replace trusting Jesus. A few years ago, I was the Keynote Speaker at a men's conference with ex-professional baseball and football player, Jay Schroeder.

Jay shared a story from his baseball days when he'd bet opposing players that he could stand at home plate and throw a baseball over the center field fence. Later, Jay led the Washington Redskins to a Super Bowl as their quarterback.

Staring at his Super Bowl ring he summed up his professional career with, "God gives each of us special talents to use for Him. I can throw things far." In that moment I knew Jay had figured out the secret to contentment was to trust Jesus with everything, especially his ability to throw things far.

KING OF PAIN

Then Moses and the Israelites sang this song to the Lord:
"I will sing to the Lord, for he is highly exalted. The horse and its rider he has hurled into the sea.
The Lord is my strength and my song; he has become my salvation.
He is my God, and I will praise him, my father's God, and I will exalt him."
~ Exodus 15:1-2

Men love being inspired. Whether by a quote, book, or song—we need inspiration. Watch any sporting event and you'll see pre-game athletes listening to their favorite tunes. Whether it's a playlist or a certain genre, music moves us. This is where it gets a little embarrassing.

As a self-absorbed teenager, my football theme song was a hit performed by The Police called, The King of Pain. It was my football go-to song.

When the song came on the radio, I'd strut around the locker room in nothing but a jock strap (remember those?) obnoxiously singing, "I'm the king of pain. I'm the king of pain."

I thought I was the coolest guy in the world. How pathetic! It's embarrassing to remember.

The public demonstration of "my song" (Exodus 15:1) was a consequence of immaturity, self-absorption, and false sense of strength.

From Exodus 15:1-2 we read God had delivered the Israelites from a seemingly helpless situation. They had no strength or purpose beyond the Egyptian mandate to work. They were a weak and pathetic people. But God rescued them. He delivered them by His strength and power. God became their strength and song.

Men, pray this with me, "Lord, release me from my worthless pride that tempts me to sing my prideful song. Set me free from my ego that rejects you and wrongly believes I can sing my own song. Amen."

TEAM MEETING FOUR:
IN THE TENT

> *"In Exodus 15 Moses and the Israelites offered sweet praises to God, but by verse 23-24 they offered bitter complaints."*
> *Anonymous*

What did you take away from last week's study and daily readings? What are you still processing? What challenged your current paradigm? What inspired you to grow as a man?

What part of your faith would you die to protect? Why? What defines your faith? What strengthens your faith more than anything else?

Let's take a look at Joshua's life so far. Who was he? What were some things he did? What is he famous for?

- He was Moses' aide:
Exodus 24:13, Numbers 11:28, and Joshua 1:1
- He was one of the spies that explored the land of Canaan:
Numbers 13:1-16 and 14:1-9
- He was the Hebrew commander in the battle against the Amalekites:
Exodus 17:8-1
- He was Moses' successor who led the Israelites into the Promised Land:
Numbers 27:12-23 and Joshua 1:1-6

From the above passages, what do we discover about Joshua's giftedness?

TEAM MEETING AT A GLANCE

- Opening Prayer, Weekly Announcements
- Personal and Victory Stories
- Each man will share his story — one man per week until all men have shared.
- After all men have shared their personal story, allow time each week for them to share victory stories.
- Weekly Study Closing Prayer
- Closing Prayer

What can we learn about his character?

So the Lord said to Moses, "Take Joshua son of Nun, a man in whom is the spirit of leadership, and lay your hand on him."
~ Numbers 27:18 (NIV)

Compare the spy report in Numbers 13:25-33 (specifically 31) with Numbers 14:6-10 (specifically 9). What separated Caleb and Joshua from the rest? What choices did they make that separated them from others?

Go to Exodus 33:7-11. In this passage we see one catalyst of greatness that Joshua possessed. What does verse 11 tell you about the greatness of Joshua's heart?

How do you interpret verse 11?

Imagine the scene in Exodus 33:7-11 as Moses walked by one million plus Hebrews watching from outside their tents as he and his aide Joshua passed by them to worship in the "tent of meeting."

Moses and Joshua entered the tent to worship God while the Jewish people worshipped with them from outside.

Jesus had something to say about meeting God. Do you have a war room? What does your "tent of meeting" look like? Do you have a place you go to pray?
Matthew 6:5-6

Did young Joshua spend more time in the tent than Moses? If so, how does time in the tent cover the spiritual leader?

What happened to the pillar of cloud (Exodus 33:9-10)? Did the cloud follow Moses when he left the tent or stand at the entrance of the tent with Joshua?

BONUS MATERIAL

Compare Joshua and Moses' responses at the crossings of the Red Sea (Exodus 14:8-31) and Jordan River (Joshua 4:1-14). What did Joshua learn from his mentor Moses?

Leaders are Learners.

From a leadership perspective, how might the song of Moses and Miriam (Exodus 15:1-21) be less effective than the stones pulled out of the Jordan River (Joshua 4:1-14)?

A good leader celebrates spiritual monuments with his people.

A great leader establishes monuments for future generations.

How did the Jordan River monument express the greatness in Joshua as a learner and leader?

Moses is dead. The Hebrew nation crossed into Promised Land and Joshua set up the monumental stones "just as Moses had directed Joshua" (10).

Joshua honored the request of his mentor even after his death.

Break into groups of three or four.

Where can you improve at meeting with God in the tent?

Take a moment today and pray for each other.

STUDY NOTES

_____

_____

_____

_____

_____

_____

_____

_____

_____

_____

_____

_____

For the next five days, read the following entries from our **The Field Guide: A Bathroom Book for Men.**

We hope they challenge and encourage you to get in the great Arena for God. See you on the Arena Floor!

FULL CAPACITY MAN

Love the Lord your God with all your heart and with all your soul and with all your strength.
~ Deuteronomy 6:5

When weightlifting, guys are notorious for measuring strength by a lift called the Bench Press. Years ago, I was doing dumbbell press sets and noticed a giant of a man named Emil staring down at me. Emil was a massive six-feet, two-inches and over 340 pounds.

When I asked what he was doing he said, "I just thought you could lift more than that." Embarrassed, I realized I hadn't been putting out the effort that matched my capacity.

God has made each of us with different capacities. Our strength is limited. We're finite beings. Capacity could be defined as how much you are. It's your potential—your life max. Just like the human brain, which operates far beneath its capacity, men often pace instead of pushing themselves.

We rest when we should run. We jog instead of sprint. God does not call us to pace ourselves, but to run at full capacity (Philippians 3:12-14). A man will never understand his full potential if he is unwilling to discover what that potential is with God in his life. God increases the capacity of a man by partnering with him.

Jesus said, "But you know him (Holy Spirit), for he lives with you and will be in you" (John 14:17).

With the conviction of God's Spirit, a man learns the art of pushing himself. He discovers his capacity by pushing the limits of his strength. As a Christian man your personal trainer "lives with you and will be in you."

How cool is that! Finish each day strong. Leave this world with zero left. Leave it all on the field. Give God your full capacity.

WORTHLESS THINGS

"If you return, then I will restore you— Before me you will stand; and if you extract the precious from the worthless, you will become my spokesman. They for their part may turn to you, but as for you, you must not turn to them. Then I will make you to this people a fortified wall of bronze; and though they fight against you they will not prevail over you; for I am with you to save you and deliver you," declares the Lord.
~ Jeremiah 15:19-20 (NASB)

One of the great disasters of our age is the pursuit of wins. Consider how much time, energy, and resources we spend on winning. How many of your pastimes are more about winning than resting? God's Sabbath is about rest not wins.

Resting is winning.

But look at us. Our worthless pursuits are pathetic. Have you thought about how worthless a win is spiritually? It's usually not the win God is after. It's the heart in the effort: win, lose, or draw.

That's why today's passage was such an epiphany when I discovered it. It redirected my focus from the worthless to the precious.

"They" in today's passage could be anyone. It could be other men, a boss, or even your pastor. God commands that if we "return" to Him, He promises to "restore" us. But returning has a price. The price is separating the "precious" or eternally valuable from the "worthless" or temporal (2 Corinthians 4:18).

Identify worthless things. They rob you of your hunger for God. Things like affluence, technology, sin, and a lifestyle that prides itself on staying busy, pull us away from God. The key is to replace those "worthless" things with the "precious" that add spiritual value.

Identify all the worthless things you need to replace in your life, and act accordingly.

ANCHORED IN THE STORM

Be strong and let us fight bravely for our people and the cities of our God. The Lord The name of the Lord is a strong tower; the righteous run to it and are safe.
~ Proverbs 18:10

Confidence is everything when backpacking into unknown terrain. Am I confident in my physical conditioning? Am I confident in my gear, partner, and outdoor skills such as finding water, making a fire, and navigating to and from destinations?

Confidence is the sustainer of courage. I once bought a cheap one-man tent and got caught in a snowstorm. I thought for sure that little tent would collapse under the weight of the fresh snow.

So many men spend their lives running toward shelters that blow down, waste away, or collapse under life's pressures. They base success on square-footage, but it's nothing more than a house of cards. During a storm a dependable shelter is the greatest need.

In life, it's also what matters most. Trust in Jesus and commit to running toward Him. Anything else will cave under the pressures of the storm. He is our anchor against the storm.

I love what Hebrews 6:19 says, "We have this hope as an anchor for the soul, firm and secure." The wise man builds a shelter over his family that stands strong under pressure. He anchors it to the Rock. It protects him in the storm.

Listen to the words of Jesus:

"Therefore everyone who hears these words of mine and puts them into practice is like a wise man who built his house on the rock. The rain came down, the streams rose, and the winds blew and beat against that house; yet it did not fall, because it had its foundation on the rock. But everyone who hears these words of mine and does not put them into practice is like a foolish man who built his house on sand. The rain came down, the streams rose, and the winds blew and beat against that house, and it fell with a great crash"
~ Matthew 7: 24-27

What is your shelter made out of ? What's it anchored to?

BAR FLIES

Woe to those who rise early in the morning to run after their drinks, who stay up late at night till they are inflamed with wine.
~ Isaiah 5:11

To celebrate Dad's sixtieth birthday, my siblings and I purchased him a guided goose hunt. Of course, Tom and I went along for moral support.

One picture from that hunt will never be forgotten. It's a picture of the three of us with limits and in red letters Dad wrote, "My hunt with Tom and Jim. The best hunt of my life."

After the hunt, Dad offered to have the geese professionally cleaned. On our way out of town we pulled into the cleaning place that happened to be located behind the local bar. Arriving at 8:00 a.m., I noticed the bar was not only opened but filled with patrons.

I said to myself, "What kind of person would be at a bar this early in the morning?"

I must've said it out loud because Tom shot back, "Anyone who works night crew and has just gotten off their shift." Tom had worked night crew for twenty years.

His was an interesting paradigm, but I still agree with Isaiah's thought in our passage for today. Drinking is a potential problem for any man. I grew up with an alcoholic grandfather and have witnessed alcoholism's effect on families. But, this passage is about more than alcohol. It's about how a man begins and ends each day.

What's the first thing you run after in the morning? Is it coffee, a relationship, or maybe your career? What about God? Where does He fit into your daily priorities?

Make it a habit to focus your early-morning attention on the things of God, not the things of self.

TANKS

For the pagans run after all these things, and your heavenly Father knows that you need them. But seek first his kingdom and his righteousness, and all these things will be given to you as well.
~ Matthew 6:32-33

Preparing for the wilderness means packing enough gear for every contingency. This means plenty of food, water, and shelter. On our New Mexico hunt "Big" Darby and I learned a valuable lesson about finding drinking water, when every topographical map ended at a dry spring, creek bed, or water trough.

Desperate to rehydrate we turned to shallow, dirt ponds known in New Mexico as tanks. Oil derricks use the tanks as holding ponds of some kind.

Using a water filter, we pumped gallons of oil-slicked water and hiked them to camp.
We survived on that water, thanks to our filters, but had a new understanding about high-octane hunting!

In our high-octane world, men are constantly on the move. We've been trained to run after the American Dream. But this high-octane dream comes at a price. Wealth toxins dilute the purity of our relationship with God.

When will we be content? We've been poisoned by a wealth that drains our spiritual passion. Too many Christian men are disconnected from the local church, being intoxicated by wealth.

Is Jesus talking about you in today's passage?

Our pagan pursuits are far worse for the spirit than the oil-slicked water we lived on for a week. And —trust me—it was gross.

Identify what toxins are polluting your faith and act accordingly. Identify the toxins you're allowing your loved ones to ingest and lead the way.

TEAM MEETING FIVE:
UNBAPTIZED ARMS

What did you take away from last week's study and daily readings? What are you still processing? What challenged your current paradigm? What inspired you to grow as a man?

How do you define greatness? What separates great men from the rest? Is there something that elevates one man to greatness while others remain mediocre?

Besides Jesus, who is the greatest man to ever live? Why do you think so? What did he do that was so special?

Unbaptized Arms. Ivan the Great was the Tsar of Russia during the Fifteenth Century. He brought together the warring tribes into one vast empire— Russia. He was a brilliant general, and a courageous fighter, who established peace across the nation.

Ivan was so busy waging his campaigns that he never married. He told his advisors that he had no time to search for a bride, but if they found a suitable one, he'd marry her.

The advisers searched the capitals of Europe and found the perfect wife for him. She was the beautiful, brilliant, and charming daughter of the King of Greece. Ivan agreed to marry her sight unseen.

The King of Greece was delighted. It would align Greece in a favorable way with the emerging giant of the north. But there had to be one condition. Ivan had to become a member of the Greek Orthodox Church and be baptized by immersion. Ivan agreed. Arrangements were concluded, and the Tsar made his way to Athens accompanied by 500 of his personal palace guard.(continued)

TEAM MEETING AT A GLANCE

- Opening Prayer, Weekly Announcements
- Personal and Victory Stories
- Each man will share his story — one man per week until all men have shared.
- After all men have shared their personal story, allow time each week for them to share victory stories.
- Weekly Study Closing Prayer
- Closing Prayer

> *"Let the world feel the weight of who I am, and let them deal with it."*
> ~ John Eldredge, Wild at Heart

His soldiers, ever loyal, asked to be baptized also, so 500 priests were assigned to give the soldiers a one-on-one catechism crash course. The soldiers, all 500 of them, were to be immersed in one mass baptism.

Crowds gathered from all over Greece. What a sight that must have been, 500 priests and 500 soldiers, a thousand men, walking into the blue Mediterranean. The priests were dressed in black robes and tall black hats, the official dress of the Orthodox Church. The soldiers wore their full battle uniforms.

But there was a problem. The Church prohibited professional soldiers from being members; they would have to give up their commitment to bloodshed. They could not be killers and church members too. So a diplomatic plan was devised.

As priests began to baptize, each soldier reached to his side and withdrew his sword. Lifting it high overhead, every soldier was totally immersed— everything baptized except his fighting arm and sword.

How does this story demonstrate times when we aren't all in for Jesus? How does it illustrate the excuses made on the way to compromise? How does compromise start?

> *"If any man seeks for greatness, let him forget greatness, and ask for truth, and he will find both."*
> ~ Horace Mann

Compromises made one choice at a time, compounded over time, become a life of compromise. **What's your take on this statement, "The full weight of who you are comes from a life totally committed to Jesus?" How can this world feel your full capacity without radical obedience to Jesus?**

Let's take a look at a man who pressed his full weight upon others— John the Baptist. Who was John and what was his mission?
Malachi 4:5, Isaiah 40:3-5, Luke 1:11-17, 35-45, and Matthew 3:1-4

John was Jesus' cousin. But he was much more than that. What did Jesus say about him?
Matthew 11:10-14

"Life is discovered when I surrender my weakness to His greatness."
~ Anonymous

Men fear the glory—being put on display. What if I fail? What if I'm humiliated? What if my motives are questioned? God wants to put His men on display. He wants to put you on display. But you need to be all-in so that you'll deflect the glory back to Him for the victories you achieve.

One step in the journey of greatness is the revelation of who you aren't. Who will you never be? What weaknesses must you embrace in order to grow in your strength?
Matthew 3:11

Another aspect of greatness is knowing who you serve. Who do you serve? Who do you trust without compromise?
John 3:22-30

He must become greater; I must become less.
~ John 3:30

> *"Do not be afraid of greatness—some are born great, some achieve greatness, and some have greatness thrust upon them."*
> ~ William Shakespeare

What makes the above statement so powerful? How did John's statement separate him from his contemporaries? How will this statement set you apart?

John 3:30 may be the greatest life verse ever spoken. John 3:22-36 in the New International Version is titled "John Testifies Again About Jesus."

What does John testify? How is his testimony different from those we hear today?

> *"We can do not great things, just small things with great love."*
> ~ Mother Teresa

How do the following verses speak to Christian greatness?
Luke 9:46-48, 22:24-30, John 12:23-25, 2 Corinthians 12:6-10, 12:9, Galatians
2:20, and 6:14

We must come to a place where God gets the credit for everything, and become the man God joyfully takes credit for. We must live immersed in Jesus— arms and all.

Where have you lifted your arms out of the water so to speak? Where do you most often rob God of His glory?

Break into groups of three or four.

Like Ivan's soldiers, what are you holding out of the water?

Where do you need to become less so He can become great?

Take a moment today and pray for each other.

> *"Surround yourself with dreamers and doers, the believers and thinkers, but most of all, surround yourself with those who see the greatness within you, even when you don't see it in yourself."*
> ~ Edmund Lee (1772-1843)

STUDY NOTES

_____

_____

_____

_____

_____

_____

_____

_____

_____

_____

_____

_____

_____

For the next five days, read the following entries from our **The Field Guide: A Bathroom Book for Men.**

We hope they challenge and encourage you to get in the great Arena for God. See you on the Arena Floor!

DEUTERONOMY 10:12 MAN

And now, O Israel, what does the Lord your God ask of you but to fear the Lord your God, to walk in all his ways, to love him, to serve the Lord your God with all your heart and with all your soul.
~ Deuteronomy 10:12

What makes a man?

Is it a six-figure income, living in the biggest home on the highest hill, or having the best toys? Men spend their lives searching for the answer, but it's not found in a bank statement. It's found in Deuteronomy 10:12, which I believe is the summit of manhood. A man is never fully a man until he embodies Deuteronomy 10:12.

The pinnacle of manhood is radical commitment to Jesus Christ. What about a man who doesn't believe?

What about him?

In his arrogance and rebellion against the Creator he'll never be the man God demands. He's a shell. He's Humpty Dumpty waiting for a fall. At best, he'll achieve finite greatness only to end in destruction.

Nothing he does will last beyond himself. Nothing. His life is a tragedy.

The Great Hunt definition of manhood was crafted as, "protecting integrity, fighting apathy, pursuing God passionately, leading courageously and finishing strong."

This definition fits all men regardless of their personal beliefs. It represents a daily journey and not something to check off of a bucket list. "Pursuing God passionately" is strategically placed at the center, representing the apex of the mountain of manhood.

Jesus is the summit of every life. Ultimate manhood begins and ends with Him.

RATTLESNAKE DANCE

...continue to work out your salvation with fear and trembling.
~ Philippians 2:12

Have you ever done the rattlesnake dance?

On more occasions than I'd like to remember I've been shaken to life by the explosion of a nearby bush and a rattler coiled to strike. You've never seen anything funnier than a grown man jumping straight in the air, screaming like a little girl, and hitting the ground dancing. Unless, that is, you're that man!

It's the rattlesnake dance.

Thinking about it sends chills up my spine.

But did you know that rattlesnakes don't rattle while hunting? They only sound off when threatened. Experts believe the rattle is a nervous warning to potential predators. It's literally a "fear and trembling" response.

Maybe God gave the snake its rattles to illustrate man's response in His presence. Don't you think the awesome power of a holy God should shake us up? It should—on a holy level—rattle us to know that one day we'll give an account for every careless word ever spoken (Matthew 12:36).

We view God too lightly don't we? We've deafened ourselves to the rattles and forgotten the venom. Sometimes we're not too far from the men in Psalm 55:19, "Who never change their ways and have no fear of God."

Change is often a response to fear, "I'm not walking up that trail ever again!" Fear can be healthy for men who've grown soft by leaning too heavily on grace. Sometimes we need to be shaken to life by God's wrath. One day knees will rattle in fear before a mighty and awesome God (Philippians 2:10).

Let the fear of God shake you up now so you won't be rattled later.

THE FEAR

If the God of my father, the God of Abraham and the Fear of Isaac, had not been with me, you would surely have sent me away empty-handed. But God has seen my hardship and the toil of my hands, and last night he rebuked you.
~ Genesis 31:42

I have many fears—the fear of falling from heights, unprotected speed, and being unsupported in deep water. But my biggest fear, however, is something you may not expect. It's being a poor steward with the life God gave me.

It's a primal fear. It should be close to the heart of men. I don't want to let God down. I don't want to face Him with fuel left in the tank.

It's my fear of fears. Do you have a fear of all fears—a fear so great that it drives your life?

Today we come to a passage that's unique in the Bible. This is one of only two times in Scripture where the word Fear is a capitalized proper noun (Genesis 31:42 and 53). What was the author of Genesis trying to convey with the "Fear of Isaac"?

In elementary school, we learned to capitalize proper nouns such as a person, place, or thing. The God of Isaac was held in such high regard that He was literally the Fear of Isaac.

In this day of soft grace, too much time is spent over-emphasizing the feminine qualities of God, and not enough on the characteristics of God's masculinity discovered in Old Testament passages dealing with God's wrath— wreaking righteous anger towards humanity.

Jesus said, "I will show you who to fear: Fear him, who after killing the body has power to throw you into hell. Yes, I tell you, fear him" (Luke 12:5).

Isaac's Fear drove him to his knees. Your Fear should drive you to yours.

Make God your greatest Fear.

Keep Him as your greatest love.

HAIL YES

Moses said to the people, "Do not be afraid; for God has come in order to test you, and in order that the fear of Him may remain with you, so that you may not sin."
~ Exodus 20:20 (NASB)

I learned about springtime Eastern Oregon lightning storms the hard way. My son James and I were using four-wheelers to move from place to place while hunting bear along the Hell's Canyon breaks. We were twelve miles from camp and unaware of the lightning storms that happened that time of year.

Out of nowhere the early afternoon erupted with marble-sized hail stones pounding the ground around us. After some discussion, we made a run for it. It must have really ticked the thunderclouds off because the sky angrily exploded. I put the pedal-to-the-metal, wrapped twelve-year-old James in an emergency tarp, and navigated through the pelting hailstones to avoid a concussion.

On the final stretch, the storm appeared to surrender, revealing an ominous rainbow wrapped in black clouds. But I was wrong. Lightning and thunder struck at point-blank range in a horrifying display of power. I pushed the pedal through the floor to outrun the explosions.

In that moment, I couldn't get far enough away from potential death by lightning. It reminded me of when the people saw the awesome display of God and, "they stayed at a distance" (Exodus 20:18).

The church today is drifting on fluffy cumulus clouds. Pastors preach of a needy God of grace desperately begging to have a relationship with His prodigal children. What about the horrifying God of the universe? What about the God who destroyed nations, flooded the earth, and sacrificed His only begotten son?

Put the pedal to the metal for that God. Fear that God. Surrender your life to that God in a holy display of awe.

FIRST NAME BASIS

Oh, that their hearts would be inclined to fear me and keep all my commands always, so that it might go well with them and their children forever!
~ Deuteronomy 5:29

Because of the years spent as a coach and player I have had tremendous respect for titles. I still address past coaches as Coach or Mister out of respect. You can imagine my surprise when I arrived at Santa Clara University as an eighteen-year-old to hear players address the coaches on a first name basis. As a Bronco, I began to understand that respect was more than a title.

On a different note, I once led a Bible study in a juvenile hall where all of the wards addressed me as "Sir." If it weren't for the prison walls they called home, you'd never know they didn't respect authority. Respect is more than words or a title. It's something earned. It's something intangible. Respect is the greatest gift one man can give another.

Listen to God's sigh in today's passage, "Oh, that their hearts would be inclined to fear me and keep all my commands always." Fearing God is more than giving Him a title. It's giving Him authority over your life. It's about total surrender. To respect God is to obey God.

Consequently, to disobey God is to disrespect Him.

Aren't you tired of flippant titles like "I'm a Christian"? Isn't it time men offer God a radically surrendered life instead of using some useless title?

Be careful about throwing around "Christian." The greatest title you can offer is a life wrapped in obedience.

Live out Romans 12:1-2, "Therefore, I urge you, brothers, in view of God's mercy, to offer your bodies as a living sacrifice, holy and pleasing to God—this is your true and proper worship. Do not conform to the pattern of this world, but be transformed by the renewing of your mind."

TEAM MEETING SIX:
UNSEEN COUNTRY

"Remember Abraham lived in a day when there wasn't a church on every corner. Heck, there weren't any churches or Bibles! Abraham's faith in God was built solely on, yep, his faith!"
Jim Ramos

What did you take away from last week's study and daily readings? What are you still processing? What challenged your current paradigm? What inspired you to grow as a man?

What's the tension between walking by faith and formulating a plan? What do you think about coach John Wooden's quote, "Failing to prepare is preparing to fail."?

Memorize this verse and its address.

> *For we walk by faith, not by sight.*
> ~ 2 Corinthians 5:7 (NASB)

In your own words, interpret 2 Corinthians 5:7. What tension is there between 2 Corinthians 5:7 and those who teach that leaders must have a clear vision and purpose? Does living by faith exclude preparation? What's the balance between faith preparation?

Leadership theory has served the church well. Thousands of books have been written on the subject. Many souls have been saved. We are told to "Play the movie" in Henry Cloud's, Nine Things you Simply Must Do, "See the end at the beginning" in The Seven Habits of Highly Effective People by Stephen Covey, and "Anyone can steer the ship but it takes a leader to chart the course," by John Maxwell in Law Four of The 21 Irrefutable Laws of Leadership.

TEAM MEETING AT A GLANCE

- Opening Prayer, Weekly Announcements
- Personal and Victory Stories
- Each man will share his story — one man per week until all men have shared.
- After all men have shared their personal story, allow time each week for them to share victory stories.
- Weekly Study Closing Prayer
- Closing Prayer

> *"Those that will deal with God must deal upon trust; we must quit the things that are seen for things that are not seen, and submit to the sufferings of this present time in hopes of a glory that is yet to be revealed."*
> ~Matthew Henry's Commentary on the Whole Bible,

On the occasions when the King James Version of the Bible is used by spiritual leaders, Proverbs 29:18a is a passage often quoted, "Where there is no vision the people perish."

In Genesis 17:5 God changed Abram's name to Abraham. How do we navigate between walking by faith, and seeing the big picture?

Is this even possible? Why is it so difficult to step out in faith when we only see part, or none, of the picture?

God sees what we don't. If we believe He is who the Bible claims, then we can trust what He sees.

Read about the "Call of Abram (Abraham)." What is it about Abram's faith that made him great? What statement might give you trouble if God called you with the words, "Go… to the land I will show you"? Discuss this passage among yourselves.
Genesis 12:1-3

Through his raw faith and ruthless trust Abram became God's friend. How are we "blessed" when we step out on faith? How does fear of failure play a role in our faith?
Isaiah 41:8-10 and James 2:23

> *"God does not tell him what land it is, that he may still cause him to walk by faith and not by sight. The apostle assures us that in all this Abram had spiritual views; he looked for a better country, and considered the land of promise only as typical of the heavenly inheritance."*
> *Adam Clarke*

Abram didn't have a Bible to read. He didn't have a pastor to offer wise counsel. He didn't have a church to choose from. There weren't Christian podcasts, Bible applications, or religious stations he could tune into for help. He had God. And that was enough.

The Lord had said to Abram, "Go from your country, your people and your father's household to the land I will show you. I will make you into a great nation, and I will bless you; I will make your name great, and you will be a blessing. I will bless those who bless you, and whoever curses you I will curse; and all peoples on earth will be blessed through you."
Genesis 12:1 (NIV)

What is the paradox between vision and faith? When is God enough? When do you struggle with trusting God when you don't have the answers?
Proverbs 29:18a (KJV), Luke 14:27-29, 2 Corinthians 4:18, 5:7, Hebrews 11:39-40, and 12:1-2

Now faith is confidence in what we hope for and assurance about what we do not see.
Hebrews 11:1 (NIV)

Faith is believing what God says and trusting your life with it. Abram's faith led him to journey to unknown lands because He believed God. What do the following verses teach about faith?
Romans 4:1-16 and Galatians 3:1-14

In the Hebrews 11 (also called the Faith Hall of Fame) there are more verses credited to Abraham than any other person; seven out of thirty-nine, with Moses coming in second with six.

By faith Abraham, when called to go to a place he would later receive as his inheritance, obeyed and went, even though he did not know where he was going.
Hebrews 11:8

As a way of sustaining this theme even further, the author has patterned the account of Abraham's call and blessing after an earlier account of a similar gift of salvation in the midst of judgment, the conclusion of the Flood narrative. The similarities between the two narratives are striking, showing that Abraham, like Noah, marks a new beginning as well as a return to God's original plan of blessing 'all mankind.'"
~ The Expositor's Bible Commentary (Pg. 111)

STUDY NOTES

_____

_____

_____

_____

_____

_____

_____

_____

_____

_____

_____

_____

For the next five days, read the following entries from our **The Field Guide: A Bathroom Book for Men.**

We hope they challenge and encourage you to get in the great Arena for God. See you on the Arena Floor!

PREDATOR MAN

But the eyes of the Lord are on those who fear him, on those whose hope is in his unfailing love.
~ Psalm 33:18

Predators are easy to spot in nature. Look at the eyes. Typical creatures of prey have eye sockets on the side of the head such as deer, elk, and antelope. Eyes are widely placed to spot predators from many angles. Peripheral vision combined with the sense of smell, hearing, and the ability to fight or flight keeps them alive.

Now, look at the eyes of a predator. You'll see sockets mounted in the front of the skull to spot and stalk prey from long distances.

Now, take a look in the mirror.

At first glance, a human's weak body, smooth skin, and long child-rearing years make man easy prey. Instead, we're the most feared animals in all creation. Why? We are made in God's image, and God has given us dominion over creation. Man is the ultimate predator, if need be. (Genesis 1:26)

God is on the hunt as well.

God is hunting for men whose hearts are fully devoted to Him. According to today's Scripture, "the eyes of the Lord are on those who fear him, on those whose hope is in his unfailing love."

Could it be that men were not made for the kill, but to hunt for something greater; to hunt for God? Could it be that the greatest quest for a man is searching for His creator?

To "hope is in his unfailing love" (Psalm 33:1) is to, "fix our eyes on Jesus the author and perfecter of our faith" (Hebrews 12:2).

Hope has the eyes of a predator. Hope is the vision of a hunter. Good hunting!

LIGHTNING ROD

The Lord confides in those who fear him; he makes his covenant known to them.
~ Psalm 25:14

In a lightning storm the best chance of safety is to make sure you're the shortest guy in the group! In fact, make sure you're not the tallest anything. Usually it's the tallest boulder, outcropping, or lone tree that acts as the lightning rod.

A lightning rod is simply a metal rod strategically placed to attract a lightning strike. It conducts lightning to the ground and away from human harm. A lightning rod protects people from danger.

Every man needs a lightning rod in his life. He needs a man who is tough enough to take the hits. I have two or three men who take my strikes, conducting them away from harm's way. These men guard my heart. They're invaluable assets in my life.

They have my back. They take my worst hits. They can handle it. I, in turn, take their hits as well.

"As iron sharpens iron, so one man sharpens another"
~ Proverbs 27:17

But there is a lightning rod that stands above the rest—Jesus. Men are limited. We're finite. Even the best man is limited in his capacity. The most reliable lightning rod is the Lord Jesus Christ. He can take your cuss words (yes, sometimes I cuss while praying), questions, and sins. Jesus stands in the gap because He cares (1 Peter 5:6-7).

He can handle your darkest moments and carry our heaviest burdens (Matthew 11:28). Be honest with God. Tell him exactly how you feel even if you use words that would make your pastor cringe. You'll never surprise God. He already knows your heart.

He is your lightning rod. He can take your hits. Shoot! He already did.

HILL TO DIE ON

You also, like living stones, are being built into a spiritual house to be a holy priesthood, offering spiritual sacrifices acceptable to God through Jesus Christ.
~ 1 Peter 2:5

In A History of Christianity, K. Scott records the famous story about Polycarp, a 2nd century bishop of Smyrna, as he was about to be burned at the stake for his faith in Christ:

When they fastened him to the stake, he said, "Leave me as I am; for he who gives me strength to sustain the fire, will enable me also, without your securing me with nails, to remain without flinching in the pile.'

Upon which they bound him without nailing him. So he said thus: 'O Father, I bless thee that thou hast counted me worthy to receive my portion among the martyrs."

The church has a saying, "The blood of the martyrs is the seed of the Church." I agree. Sacrifice inspires. Ask yourself, "Is this the hill I am willing to die on?"

Some things grip us with such conviction that we're willing to lose everything to hold them. Someone once said, "An opinion is something you hold. A conviction is something that holds you."

Often, that conviction holds us to the cross we carry up the hill we eventually die on. But isn't it worth it? Some hills aren't worthy of our blood, sweat, and tears. Yet for others we'll gladly put the cross on our shoulders and start climbing. The sacrifices of the saints are the bricks in the house of God. The mortar of sacrifice binds the

Kingdom of God. It's the seed of the Church.

Sacrifice binds men together. Men rally around a common purpose often in the form of sacrifice. What hill will you die on? What great cause will you sacrifice your life for to glorify God?

IN VELVET

Seek the Lord while he may be found; call on him while he is near.
~ Isaiah 55:6

July is one of my favorite months of the year. The sun is out, our Oregon days are long, and hunting season is rapidly approaching. Bucks and bulls are in full velvet and spend more time in the open to protect their sensitive antlers.

But once the velvet is rubbed off and their antlers harden, they disappear into their secluded world of brush and timber. If you want to go scout these magnificent creatures, summer is the time to watch wildlife in their most casual state.

Our time on earth is much like scouting season. It's a precursor of what's to come. Time on earth is short. The opportunity is short so, "seek the Lord while he may be found" (Isaiah 55:6).

Because, as Hebrews 9:27 warns, "It is appointed for men to die once and after this comes the judgment." (NASB)

This is our time. This is our season.

This is our opportunity to seek the Lord. Upon death, the reality of a man's seeking will be rewarded —either to eternal separation or union with the Creator of the Universe. In heaven, there will be a constant connection with our King. But our time on earth is where we learn the art of hunting for God.

In his life-changing book Heaven, Randy Alcorn writes, "For the believer, earth is the closest we will ever get to hell, but for the unbeliever earth is the closest they will ever get to heaven."

Seek God now. Seek Him before it's too late for you.

BORED MEETINGS

And without faith it is impossible to please God, because anyone who comes to him must believe that he exists and that he rewards those who earnestly seek him.
~ Hebrew 11:6

It was only one week into the archery season and—I confess—I was completely unmotivated. For the first time in my life I wasn't excited about hunting. I'd simply lost the passion to chase unseen animals up and down mountains.

Furthermore, I wasn't journaling my daily Bible studies. And, my morning prayer times were getting further and further apart. In a word, I was bored with life and my routine was suffering for it.

After some soul searching, I discovered that my boredom was the result of not keeping first things first. For an unknown reason I'd put God on the back burner and everything else was suffering because of it. From that I learned two things about faith that inspired me to "earnestly seek him."

First, faith begins with the realization that God exists as the only uncreated being in the Universe. God came from nowhere. He wasn't created. He simply is. When God says, "I am" (Exodus 3:14) He means it. Before anything else, God existed. It blows my mind.

Second, according to Hebrews 11:6, "he rewards those who earnestly seek him."
It's not good enough to "believe that he exists."

"Even the demons believe that — and shudder" (James 2:19).

Faith must move us into a new realm. Faith responds to God's existence when we "earnestly seek."
It's only when a man earnestly seeks Him that his faith is activated. Faith is activated by our pursuit (Matthew 6:33). An active faith results in the ride of our life. It's a ride that's never boring and never ending as we continue to pursue God.

Get out of the rut you're in by chasing after your God.

TEAM MEETING SEVEN:
THE SERVANT'S TOWEL

> *"Every man must decide whether he will walk in the light of creative altruism or in the darkness of destructive selfishness."*
> ~ Martin Luther King Jr.

What did you take away from last week's study and daily readings? What are you still processing? What challenged your current paradigm? What inspired you to grow as a man?

I became a man as a twenty-eight-year-old pastor after a Promise Keepers event in the Los Angeles Coliseum when I decided to out-love and out-serve Shanna. Today's focus is on the servant mindset of Jesus, the ultimate man, and how to set aside personal ambitions and ego long enough to discover that true manhood comes through serving others.

Each of us will have a chance to answer the following: What is ambition and where are you the most ambitious?

At what point does ambition become an issue of ego, conceit, and selfishness? How do you regulate the tension between ambition and arrogance? How does serving others act as a governor over selfishness?

How has your ambition hurt you? Who else has it hurt? Who bears the wounds because of your ambition?

TEAM MEETING AT A GLANCE

- Opening Prayer, Weekly Announcements
- Personal and Victory Stories
- Each man will share his story — one man per week until all men have shared.
- After all men have shared their personal story, allow time each week for them to share victory stories.
- Weekly Study Closing Prayer
- Closing Prayer

> *"When ambition ends, happiness begins."*
> ~ Thomas Merton

Let's look at Jesus' last night before being tortured to death in John 13:1- 17 titled, Jesus Washes His Disciples' Feet. Will someone please read this passage out loud? The passage below is where we got the title of today's meeting.

> *Jesus knew that the Father had put all things under his power, and that he had come from God and was returning to God; so he got up from the meal, took off his outer clothing, and wrapped a towel around his waist. After that, he poured water into a basin and began to wash his disciples' feet, drying them with the towel that was wrapped around him.*
> ~ John 13:3-5

Did you know that the military word sergeant comes from the Latin, meaning servant?

What other insights do you see in this passage? Did you notice he washed Judas' feet moments before Judas left to betray him (John 13:30)? What did Jesus mean in verses 12-17? Whose feet are you washing, and in what way? Where have you put on the servant's towel?

> *"Don't push your way to the front; don't sweet talk your way to the top. Put yourself aside, and help others get ahead. Don't be obsessed getting your own advantage. Forget yourselves long enough to lend a helping hand."*
> ~ Philippians 2:3-4, The Message Paraphrase

> *"We cannot seek achievement for ourselves and forget about progress and prosperity for our community... Our ambitions must be broad enough to include the aspirations and needs of others, for their sakes and for our own."*
> ~ Cesar Chavez

Take a look at John 13:17. What did Jesus mean by, "Now that you know these things, you will be blessed if you do them."? How has serving others brought happiness and fulfillment into your life? How has putting on the servant's towel blessed you? What secret to happiness do we see in serving others?

What in your life needs to die for you to be a more selfless man? Read John 12:24-25 (below) and put Jesus' words into your own. What life lesson is Jesus teaching? What do the following Bible passages teach us about dying to self?
Luke 9:21-24, Galatians 2:20, 6:14, and Philippians 1:20-22

> *"Great ambition is the passion of a great character. Those endowed with it may perform very good or very bad acts. All depends on the principles which direct them."*
> ~ Napoleon Bonaparte

"Truly truly I say to you, unless a grain of wheat falls into the earth and dies, it remains alone; but if it dies, it bears much fruit. He who loves his life loses it, and he who hates his life in this world will keep it to life eternal."
~ John 12:24-25

The propensity of selfishness is to resurrect itself even after we kill it. Essentially, we must die to self daily. What does the Bible teach about how to do this?
Romans 12:1-2, 13:8-10, Galatians 5:13-14, 6:1-3, and Philippians 2:3-4 (below)

Do nothing out of selfish ambition or vain conceit.
Rather, in humility value others above yourselves, not looking to your own interests but each of you to the interests of the others.
~ Philippians 2:3-4

> *"Almost every sinful action ever committed can be traced back to a selfish motive. It is a trait we hate in other people but justify in ourselves."*
> ~ Stephen Kendrick, The Love Dare

Have you identified a blind spot? Have you discovered a chink in your armor? Can you recognize your own passivity? Where do you need to overcome your self ? Where do you need to set yourself aside and serve others?

> *"Above all the grace and the gifts that Christ gives to his beloved is that of overcoming self."*
> ~ St. Francis of Assisi

Ambition isn't always a bad thing. But when it becomes self-serving and narcissistic it must be repented of in order to serve others in love. As men, we must put the needs of others above our own. When our ambitions veer from Biblical truth then we need to turn around and follow Jesus to the cross.
Matthew 20:26-28, John 3:16, Romans 5:7-9, 1 Timothy 2:5-7, Hebrews 9:15, and 1 Peter 2:24

Break into groups of three or four.

Share one thing you need to crucify: What one thing can you tackle today in order to defeat selfishness?

Who have you neglected to serve?

Is there a need in your local church you can meet?

Take a moment today and pray for each other,

> *"The mark of the immature man is that he wants to die nobly for a cause, while the mark of the mature man is that is wants to live humbly for one."*
> ~ Wilhelm Stekel

STUDY NOTES

_____

_____

_____

_____

_____

_____

_____

_____

_____

_____

_____

_____

For the next five days, read the following entries from our **The Field Guide: A Bathroom Book for Men.**

We hope they challenge and encourage you to get in the great Arena for God. See you on the Arena Floor!

QUEST FOR GLORY

He will render to each one according to his works: to those who by patience in well-doing seek for glory and honor and immortality, he will give eternal life; but for those who are self-seeking and do not obey the truth, but obey unrighteousness, there will be wrath and fury
~ Romans 2:6-8 (ESV)

I proudly displayed dozens of trophies that filled an eight-foot church table, explaining how each was earned—none were participation trophies. The students sat mesmerized as I explained, "These are my back-to-back Athlete of the Year trophies, and this one is for the Most Courageous on my Santa Clara football team." I continued, story after story.

When I finished, I lifted the table and the trophies crashed to the floor in an explosion of metal, marble, wood, and plastic. My students got the point.

There's a quest for glory in every man. Even after the cheers have stopped, stadiums have emptied, and the memories are forgotten—we continue to talk about our trophies.

True "glory, honor and immortality" (Romans 2:6-8) however, is not found in our worldly pursuit of triumph. It's found in the quest for eternity. The Bible teaches that man is God's greatest trophy, and He demands reciprocation on our part.

Verse 8 talks about men "who are selfishly ambitious" (NASB) — seeking personal glory.

These men have lost sight of eternity. They've tried to capture the glory for themselves, but their glory is only temporary. Their light is a paper fire at best. Their trophies will come crashing in a glorious display at the end of their days.

So, what's the point?

Pursue the right trophies. Pursue the trophies that are eternally stamped. Pursue the glory that never crashes.

HUME LAKE

My heart says of you, "Seek his face!" Your face, Lord, I will seek.
~ Psalm 27:8

Over a twenty-year span as a youth pastor, I took students from California and Oregon to Hume Lake Christian Camps. It's a beautiful place with an overwhelming Presence that drew me in by its crisp Sierra Nevada air, smell of pine, and the sounds of mallard ducks, frogs, and wildlife. God has used Hume Lake to change thousands of lives and I, admittedly, am one of them.

For many it was a speaker, band, counselor, or injury incurred during Hume's famous Rec Time that God used to get their attention. For me, God's glorious creation pulled me into His presence. Men are drawn to something great—something greater than themselves.

The heart of man is drawn to the face of God, but so many follow counterfeit paths to an unfulfilled life (John 10:10) leading them nowhere. But there is one trail, obscure and hidden, that leads to the Creator of the Universe.

The Psalmist wrote, "My heart says of you, 'Seek his face'" (Psalm 27:8).

But, what does it mean to seek God's face? What does His face represent?

God has offered His face as a target, but what does it mean?

God's face represents His truth, character, and nature. I'm drawn to Hume Lake because of God's "invisible attributes, His eternal power and divine nature have been clearly seen, being understood through what has been made" (Romans 1:20).

God's invisible nature through His visible creation has been revealed to mankind.
This is the place where God's handiwork screams. And I will listen. I will seek His face.

BREAKFAST TABLE

O God, you are my God, earnestly I seek you; my soul thirsts for you, my body longs for you, in a dry and weary land where there is no water.
~ Psalm 63:1

I've forgotten many past hikes, but one will never be forgotten. While hiking on a hot summer day at Hume Lake, I ran into a buck-naked man wearing nothing except yellow socks, penny loafers, and a fedora hat—true story! It was an awkward moment to say the least.

It was like spotting a Sasquatch, only worse! I hope he had on his sunscreen!

I appropriately named that eight-mile loop The Naked Man Trail. Hiking it became an annual event at Hume Lake for the students in our youth group, but high altitude combined with intense heat was always challenging for us wet-weather Oregonians.

Reflecting back to that scorching day on The Naked Man Trail, I can appreciate what the psalmist meant when he reflected on a "dry and weary land where there is no water."

In Psalm 63:1 the word "earnestly" literally means "early." Isn't it interesting? Science tells us that breakfast is the most important meal of the day and actually lengthens the human life. After a night of being fast asleep our bodies need to replenish. The human system is replenished when we break our fast with food.

In the same way, the soul that truly "thirsts" and "longs for" God is the soul that must be replenished with Christ—early. Hunger is satisfied when we choose to come to God's table.

Make time at God's table a core value in your life. Commit to God daily with prayer and Bible reading.

How long can you spiritually fast before you partake of Christ? When do you feast on God? At what point does your thirst for Him become unquenchable?

GREAT FOR GOOD

But seek first his kingdom and his righteousness, and all these things will be given to you as well.
~ Matthew 6:33

As a child I collected knives, baseball cards, arrowheads, coins, stamps, rattlesnake rattles, deer antlers, comic books, old fishing reels, beer steins, guns, and stamps. You name it, and I probably collected it. It was my introduction to American consumerism. Collecting was a form of consuming for this elementary school kid.

Men are collectors. We're conquerors. We collect the next win to notch on our belt. We'll chase anything that's a challenge or potential conquest. Maybe that's why women are so intriguing. Their mystery keeps us coming back for more. After more than two decades I'm still pursuing Shanna's mystery.

We were created for the hunt. Men will run after what's behind that tape stretched across a finish line. Men, however, often waste life pursuing the wrong things. Great men became average by compromising their quest of greatness for good things.

Jesus said, "God blesses those who are humble for they will inherit the whole earth" (Matthew 5:5 NLT). The humble in Jesus pursue something more, different— something of great value. The humble inherit the blessings of Heaven because their pursuit is for the Great One instead of good things.

Good is the enemy of great.

The good pursuit of wealth is the enemy of greatness if it compromises "knowing Christ." Our most passionate pursuit should be to "seek first his kingdom and his righteousness" (Matthew 6:33).

The greatest hunt of all is the pursuit of the Great One.

KILLER

But if from there you seek the Lord your God, you will find him if you look for him with all your heart and with all your soul.
~ Deuteronomy 4:29

I have a friend who is an expert marksman with a rifle. He loves to shoot, reloads most of his ammunition, and talks shop with the best of them. I've known him two decades and he's only taken one big game animal to date. After hunting with him I found out why. He's afraid of the dark. Shoot, he's generally afraid of the outdoors.

He might be a hunter, but he's not a killer. There is a huge difference.

Hunters don't put out the effort to find game. They enjoy the camp life, hanging out around the fire, drinking a beer, and sleeping until sunrise. They're in camp for the camaraderie and the experience. And that's okay—unless of course—you want to kill something.

They carry the wonderful smells of camp with them, but have neglected the fact that when animals see, smell, or hear humans they hide.

Here's the takeaway. God hides too. He's not desperate. He doesn't beg. He doesn't need you. He doesn't bless casual pursuit or half-hearted devotion.

You can hunt for God, but finding Him takes a Jeremiah 29:13 effort, "You will seek me and find me when you seek me with all your heart."

How badly do you want God? How hungry are you? The psalmist wrote, "As the deer pants for streams of water, so my soul pants for you, O God. My soul thirsts for God, for the living God. When can I go and meet with God" (Psalm 42:1-2)?

Unlike beasts in the field, God doesn't hide from us. He hides for us. He wants men to diligently seek Him. This Trophy, the pursuit of God, is worthy of a man's best effort.

TEAM MEETING EIGHT:
WITNESS STADIUM

> *"Live as the kind of man that makes Jesus stand to cheer you on."*
> ~ Anonymous

What did you take away from last week's study and daily readings? What are you still processing? What challenged your current paradigm? What inspired you to grow as a man?

Share about an event you witnessed that inspired the crowd to stand and cheer. What made this moment so special?

It's awesome to get caught up in the same moment with hundreds and thousands of people filling a stadium, sharing an inspiring moment.

When is it appropriate to give a standing ovation and when is it not?

Stand in recognition of a great moment not a great man—unless that man is Jesus.

Men are drawn to great stadiums hoping to witness great men do great things. Maybe they're on the hunt for something not too far from the truth. Read about the ultimate venue— Witness Stadium.

84

TEAM MEETING AT A GLANCE

- Opening Prayer, Weekly Announcements
- Personal and Victory Stories
- Each man will share his story — one man per week until all men have shared.
- After all men have shared their personal story, allow time each week for them to share victory stories.
- Weekly Study Closing Prayer
- Closing Prayer

> *"The church owes Paul to the prayer of Stephen."*
> ~ Augustine

Therefore, since we are surrounded by such a great cloud of witnesses, let us throw off everything that hinders and the sin that so easily entangles. and let us run with perseverance the race marked out for us, fixing our eyes on Jesus, the pioneer and perfecter of our faith, who for the joy set before him endured the cross, scorning its shame, and sat down at the right hand of the throne of God.

How do you interpret Hebrews 12:1-2? What stands out the most for you?

No one knows for sure if there's an actual Witness Stadium in Heaven, but we do know that someone is watching our faith race on earth. If there's an actual Witness Stadium, then who fills the stands?
Hebrews 11:35-40 and Revelation 2:13

Hebrews 11 is referred to as the "Faith Hall of Fame." Its verses are filled with men and women of faith who lived and died, never witnessing the coming of the Messiah—Jesus.

The Greek word martyr, *martureo*, means witness. It was used in the secular sphere as well as in the New Testament. The process of bearing witness was not intended to lead to death, but witnesses for Jesus often died for their testimonies.

With this concept of Witness Stadium in mind let's spend the rest of our time looking at "The Stoning of Stephen" in Acts 7:54-60.

"The main problem in this section is the nature of Stephen's death. He had been tried by the Sanhedrin (Jewish Court), but that body had no power to put anybody to death (John 18:31)."
~ Tyndale New Testament Commentaries

What can we learn about Stephen? What separated him from the pack?
Acts 6:1-15

In Acts 7:1-53 Stephen makes a convincing, yet futile, argument in his defense. What strikes you interesting in Acts 7:55-8:1? Where is Jesus' typical posture in heaven?
Psalm 110:1, Matthew 26:64, Colossians 3:1, Hebrews 12:2, Revelations 5:13, 6:16, 7:10, and 15, Revelation 5:6-8 and 14:1-5 are the only other times Jesus stands in heaven.

Why do you think Jesus stood at Stephen's death?
Matthew 10:32-33 and Revelation 3:5

"So you too, when you do all the things which are commanded you, say, 'We are unworthy slaves; we have done only that which we ought to have done.'"
~ Luke 17:10 (NASB)

> *"Stephen has been confessing Christ before men, and now he sees Christ confessing Stephen before God. The proper posture of a witness is the standing posture. Stephen, condemned by an earthly court, appeals for vindication to a heavenly court, and his vindicator in that Supreme Court is Jesus, who stands at God's right hand as Stephen's advocate."*
> ~ F.F. Bruce, Book of Acts pg. 168

Paul also stood at Stephen's death, but his motives were quite different from Jesus'.
Acts 22:19-21

Imagine Witness Stadium filled with a myriad of the great men and women of faith watching Stephen's death. Suddenly all eyes turn to Jesus as he stands in honor of the man honoring Him with his death—Stephen. Silently all seats empty as witnesses stand in reverence of Stephen's good and worthy martyrdom. But their silence turns to waves of applause as Stephen cries out, "Lord Jesus, receive my spirit. Lord, do not hold this sin against them."

Does Stephen deserve any credit for Paul's salvation? How might Stephen's death have haunted Paul?
Acts 8:1-3 and 1 Corinthians 15:3-9

"The religious are on a never-ending crusade against the righteousness."
~ Unknown

How will you live and die on this earth in such a way as to make Jesus stand?
Matthew 25:14-30 and Luke 17:7-10

Live in such a way that causes Jesus to stand. Make your life goal to honor Him. One day you will see Him face to face. Imagine breathing your last breath on this dark planet after scratching, clawing, and battling for your King. You're bruised and bloodied from the fray, crawling on all fours, exhausted, only to have two nail-scarred hands reach out to you and lift you slowly, tenderly, to eye level.

Seeing your Master eye to eye, you begin to weep, the tears flowing down your marred face. Like a loving father he wipes the tears from your eyes and says, "Well done my good and faithful servant."

> *"However hard he tried Saul could never forget the way in which Stephen had died. The blood of the martyrs even thus early had begun to be the seed of the church."*
> ~ William Barclay

"Saul was right there congratulating the killers."
~ Acts 8:1 The Message Paraphrase

Let's tackle verse 10. Compare Proverbs 27:10, "Better a neighbor nearby than a brother far away" with Proverbs 18:24, "One who has unreliable friends soon comes to ruin, but there is a friend who sticks closer than a brother." What are your thoughts?

Relationships see the context of our situations. Proximity sees more clearly than the long-distance relationship.

How do you understand verse 10: "Do not go to your brother's house when disaster strikes you —better a neighbor nearby than a brother far away"?

Which of these statements is true? "Better a neighbor nearby than a brother far away" or "Blood is thicker than water?"

- "Kin-blood is not spoilt by water." Heinrich der Glîchezære (1180)
- "Blood is thicker than water." John Ray (1670)

Finish the sentence: I'm the kind of friend that _____

Here's a funny story about a friend who did not have his friend's back:

Two adventurous teenage boys were out exploring when they came upon a set of large bear tracks. They decided to follow the tracks, moving with extreme caution. Suddenly, from behind a rock, jumped a giant Grizzly bear. Standing squarely in front of them, the bear beat on his chest and roared, its' terrible sounds echoing off the canyon walls.

Horrified, the two boys turned to run for their lives. Just then, one of the boys dropped to the floor and started untying his heavy hiking boots. He whipped the boots off, jammed on his running shoes, and began tying the laces. His friend yelled, "Come on, man! Let's get out of here! Why in the world are you changing shoes? We don't have much of a chance of outrunning that bear anyway!" Lunging to his feet, the first boy replied, "I don't have to outrun that bear. All I have to do is outrun you!"

> *"Keep your friends close and your enemies closer."*
> ~ Secular Proverb

Men have a tendency to isolate themselves from got-your-back relationships with other men. This is not only unwise but dangerous. Why do you need at least one man like this in your life?

Break into groups of three or four.

Who's back do you have? Why? Would they agree? Who's got your back?

Pray for those people.

Take a moment today and pray for each other.

> *"The soul is sweetened by the good counsels of a friend."*
> ~ Latin translation

STUDY NOTES

_____

_____

_____

_____

_____

_____

_____

_____

_____

_____

_____

_____

For the next five days, read the following entries from our **The Field Guide: A Bathroom Book for Men.**

We hope they challenge and encourage you to get in the great Arena for God. See you on the Arena Floor!

LABRADOR HEART

My flesh and my heart may fail, but God is the strength of my heart and my portion forever.
~ Psalm 73:26

I've had a Labrador retriever in my home for most of my adult life. What I love the most about this breed is their unwavering desire to please their master—in this case me. I've heard of Labs literally running themselves to death to please their master. If you want a dog with heart, choose a Labrador and you won't be disappointed.

They are pure to the core. It's who they are.

The heart is man's core—it's who he is. It's his essence. It's his source.

Every word he speaks flows from his heart (Matthew 12:34-36). Every motivation, dream, and ambition flows from the deep source of the heart (Psalm 37:4). Religion attempts to change the outside of a man, but Jesus replaces our heart of stone with a heart of flesh (Ezekiel 11:19, 36:26). Jesus demands Labrador-like commitment from His men. He requires all of your heart (Deuteronomy 6:4-5).

All of it.

Today's verse forces the question, "How much of my heart really trusts in God? Is God truly my portion or just a portion of my portion?"

"God is the strength of my heart and my portion forever" speaks of rhythm. It speaks of the movement between a man and his God. It's easy for men to rely on knowledge, strength, and abilities instead of on God.

True godliness relies on something much deeper. The godly man's portion is found in the strength that only comes from keeping in perfect rhythm with God (Galatians 5:23).

Reflect on your heart daily. How much did God get today? How much did I steal from Him? Today give Him your portion, not a portion of your portion.

FEAST ON IT

So David and his men wept aloud until they had no strength left to weep... But David found strength in the LORD his God.
~ 1 Samuel 30:4 and 6

Describing the modern church, John Maxwell said, "In Acts chapter two they prayed for ten days, Peter preached for ten minutes and 3,000 were saved. Today, churches pray for ten minutes, preach for thirty days and three get saved."

Now that's a statement to ponder.

Years ago, I embarked on a quest to interview pastors in an attempt to learn more about my profession. I composed a list of questions and pastors. One question was, "Can you tell me about your devotional life?"

It wasn't meant to be a compass, but I was shocked at what I discovered. Of the twenty men, all pastors, only one had a consistent time with the Lord in the morning that included Bible study and prayer.

One.

No wonder the Church struggles. No wonder men fail. How can men know the Word of God better than anyone of his family when their pastor is indifferent to it?

Isn't the goal of spiritual leadership to "go and make disciples" (Matthew 28:19)?

If men rely on their pastor to warm up the milk, they'll be greatly disappointed. Imagine men, nursing off their pastors' breasts each week instead of learning to feed on their own. But this is exactly what happens when the Word of God is neglected. When you're indifferent to the Word of God, you remain a spiritual baby; "You need milk, not solid food" (Hebrews 5:12).

David "strengthened himself in the Lord his God." Do the same. A good rule is God's daily bread before your daily bread. Feast on God's Word before you feast on anything else.

TUCK, CURL, AND PRAY

I love you, O Lord, my strength. The Lord is my rock, my fortress and my deliverer; my God is my rock, in whom I take refuge. He is my shield and the horn of my salvation, my stronghold.
~ Psalm 18:1-2

I'll never forget the sight of a boulder, high up on Mt. Whitney's summit, shattered by a lightning strike. Summiting only moments before a pending lightning storm, we raced down the mountain to avoid looking like that shattered boulder. At the bottom of the mountain, a wise old mountain man shared his lightning storm rule, "Tuck into a ball, curl up under the largest rock you can find—and pray."

His advice reminds me of another wise guy who once joked about lightning storms, "Stick your head between your legs and kiss your butt goodbye."

I bet David was familiar with hiding behind rocks and ducking into caves while evading Saul's murderous threats (1 Samuel 24:1-7).

Imagine David's memories reflected upon the months of hiding from Saul's wrath. We know of at least once when David looked up to those steep crags and reflected, "I look to the hills— where does my help come from. My help comes from the Lord" (Psalm 121:1-2).

When I think of God as my rock and deliverer, I think of the God who is steadfast and resolute, "the same yesterday and today and forever" (Hebrews 13:8).

I think of the God a man can hide under when there's nowhere else to turn (1 Peter 5:6-7). I think of the God who gives us confidence in any and every circumstance (Philippians 4:12-13).

"He alone is my rock and my salvation" (Psalm 62:2).

BENCH PRESS SHIRT

The Lord reigns, he is robed in majesty; the Lord is robed in majesty and is armed with strength. The world is firmly established; it cannot be moved.
~ Psalm 93:1

I was in the men's locker room when I overheard some guys talking about their bench press. I couldn't help hearing one guy boast of benching close to five hundred pounds. He mentioned that he "maxed" better when he wore "The Shirt."

I learned that the Bench Press Shirt is a compression shirt designed to restrict motion in the upper body by limiting joint movement while compressing the muscles. Essentially, the Bench Press Shirt adds strength to a normally weaker man. It hit me. Jesus is our Bench Press Shirt.

Listen to this: "I am going to send you what my Father has promised; but stay in the city until you have been clothed with power from on high" (Luke 24:49).

Check out this description of Jesus, "For in him all things were created: things in heaven and on earth, visible and invisible, whether thrones or powers or rulers or authorities; all things have been created through him and for him. He is before all things, and in him all things hold together" (Colossians 1:16-17). (NIV)

Jesus is our source of power. But we must put on Jesus.

God is strength.

Just as God is love (1 John 4:8), God is strength. Strength can't be removed from God without making Him less than God. The man who trusts God puts on the strength of the universe.

Doesn't that sound much better than a Bench Press Shirt?

WAY OF THE SHOOTER

Look to the LORD and his strength; seek his face always.
~ Psalm 105:4

Author Aldo Leopold rightly said, "A trophy is measured in effort not inches." Hunting is becoming a rich man's sport, but there's more to taking a trophy than pulling the trigger. Men pay high dollars for hunts that end way before the trigger is pulled. Guides often call themselves professional hunters and their clients' shooters, reserving the former term for themselves.

The guide is the real hunter.

The guide does all the work while the client pulls the trigger. Successful, yes, but clients soon become soft, having forgotten the joy of battling the challenges of the wild and returning home with a great trophy that's measured much more in effort than inches.

Shooters have forgotten the most important thing; the great fulfillment in pushing one's body to its limits and doing something on their own—even if that means failure.
Worse, however, are the men who hunt for the wrong things. Men are made to pursue trophies. But trophies are elusive. It takes strength for the man to devote his life as a Godhunter in a world of shooters who do little to pursue God besides listening to a weekly pulpit filler.

When will we realize the sheer joy of a life spent chasing the greatest Trophy of all? Hunt for God in the wild. Don't take the easy, guided tour.

Don't follow the shooter's way.

Philippians 3:13-14, "But one thing I do: Forgetting what is behind and straining toward what is ahead, I press on toward the goal to win the prize for which God has called me heavenward in Christ Jesus."

TEAM MEETING NINE;
THE WINE PRESS

"God is not as concerned with us as he is with you."
~ Anonymous

What did you take away from last week's study and daily readings? What are you still processing? What challenged your current paradigm? What inspired you to grow as a man?

Imagine that you are holding yourself prisoner. What cage are you in? What is preventing you from being the man God created you to be?

Which of the following nine statements most describes the cage preventing you from being the man God has created you to become?

- I'm too old for that anymore. I passed the baton of serving in the church to the younger guys.
- I'll just throw money at the problem and hope nobody knows that I'm trapped in the comforts of my wealth.
- I'm a mature believer and have known God for many years. There is nothing anyone else can offer me.
- I have too many problems. My marriage is a mess. My kids are struggling. I'm totally stressed out. I'm not in a place to serve God, let alone others.
- I'm too busy with my career. Maybe when I retire and things slow down I'll step out in faith.

TEAM MEETING AT A GLANCE

- Opening Prayer, Weekly Announcements
- Personal and Victory Stories
- Each man will share his story — one man per week until all men have shared.
- After all men have shared their personal story, allow time each week for them to share victory stories.
- Weekly Study Closing Prayer
- Closing Prayer

> *"When we look at ourselves in the wine press we need to realize that we are warriors of the King. When we realize how great God is we will begin to realize how great we are and say, 'I am a mighty warrior!' God sees beyond the wine press to what you and He can conquer together.*
> ~ Anonymous

- I have a secret world of sin that no one knows about. I'm not even living for Jesus right now. I know all the church talk, and how to smile on Sundays, but my faith is lukewarm at best.
- If I get radical for Jesus life won't be fun and exciting anymore. I don't want to be less of a man by being some Jesus freak.
- Do you want to break me down? All right, I'm afraid. I'm afraid I might fail. I'm afraid I'll be mocked. I'm afraid my motives will be questioned.
- I don't know enough. I've only been a follower of Jesus a short time. I'm nobody. I have very little education. I'm not talented. I'm not the smartest apple in the bush. Or, do apples grow on trees? See, I told you. It won't be hard for God to find someone better.

Why are men so resistant (stubborn might be a better word) when God calls out their greatness? Why do we act like God is wrong in His view of us? What can you become great at if you stepped out in faith?

"Gideon is a judge of the Israelites who wins a decisive victory over a Midianite army with a vast numerical disadvantage, leading a troop of three hundred men."
~ Wikipedia

Now we're going to look at the call of Gideon. Gideon has some major insecurities to overcome. Even after God calls him, Gideon tests Him to confirm it. Take turns reading this amazing story.
Judges 6:1-40

"The ancient wine press consisted of a shallow vat, built above ground or excavated in the rock and, through holes in the bottom, communicating with a lower vat also frequently excavated in the rock. From the upper vat the juice trickled into the lower.
Ordinarily they consisted of two rectangular or circular excavations, hewn in the solid rock to a depth of 2 or 3 feet. Where possible one was always higher than the other and they were connected by a pipe or channel.
Their size, of course, varied greatly, but the upper vat was always wider and shallower than the lower and was the press proper, into which the grapes were thrown and crushed by the feet of the treaders. The juice flowed down through the pipe into the lower vat, from which it was removed into jars or where it was allowed to remain during the first fermentation."
~ The International Standard Bible Encyclopedia

Imagine the scene in Judges 6:11-12. Gideon is hiding from the Midianites in a two to three-foot-tall wine press while threshing wheat! It must have been quite a spectacle! But what did God see? How was Gideon's view of himself different from God's?

Manasseh was the oldest son of Joseph. He was born in Egypt, his mother being Asenath, daughter of Potiphera, priest of On. In race he and his brother Ephraim were half Hebrew and half Egyptian. Subsequently, when listing the Twelve Tribes of Israel there are thirteen names mentioned. Joseph's tribe is listed as two half portions—Ephraim and Manasseh.

When Jacob was nearing his death, he desired to bless the two boys (Genesis 48:5-20). Joseph took Ephraim in his right hand, facing Jacob's left, and Manasseh in his left, facing Jacob's right. But the dying patriarch crossed his arms, laying his right hand on Ephraim's head and his left on Manasseh's.

Prophetically speaking although both sons should become ancestors of great peoples, Ephraim should excel. This is why Ephraim, the younger son, is always listed ahead of Manasseh, making Manasseh the lesser of the two.

First God deconstructs Gideon's identity, and then destroys his plans?
How did Gideon respond? Put yourself in his shoes.
How might you respond?
Judges 6:13-15

> *"I have seen the enemy and he is us!"*
> ~ Pogo (comic strip)

Gideon was from the smallest of all tribes in Israel—the half-tribe of Manasseh. His clan was the smallest of Manasseh's. He was also the weakest man in the family. The tension of stepping out in radical trust is that we, like Gideon, only see ourselves today—the now. But God sees the potential in the man He's created—the then.

> *"Pardon me, my lord," Gideon replied, "but how can I save Israel? My clan is the weakest in Manasseh, and I am the least in my family."*
> ~ Judges 6:15 (NIV)

In Judges 6:13-14 Gideon's uses six "us" statements to defer God's call on his life? God rebuts Gideon with two "you" statements. By verse 15 Gideon acknowledges (but doesn't accept the call) with his "I" and "my" statements.

Why do we defer leadership to others such as our wife, children, and pastors instead of accepting responsibility?

Men don't defer. Males do.

What does God ask from us? What doesn't He ask? Why is this important for us to understand?
Judges 6:14

God never asks you to give what you don't have. All He wants is all you have.

Gideon stopped hiding. In Judges 6:18, still troubled by his call, Gideon stepped out of the wine press! Read the rest of the chapter and discuss the process to God that Gideon went through. Why is taking small steps in obedience so important in discovering God's mission?
Judges 6: 19-30, Deuteronomy 6:5, Matthew 22:36-38 and Luke 16:10

> *"Be careful that your wine press does not become your whine press."*
> ~ Anonymous

> *"Your attitude determines your altitude."*
> ~ John Maxwell

Where are you the most insecure in your ability? Why is it so tough for men to see God's authority on them? Where is your greatness hiding in some wine press?
2 Corinthians 4:13, 18, 1 Samuel 16:7, 2 Chronicles 16:9, and Matthew 11:12

Take time this week and conduct an Internet search on the character and nature of God. Pray over God's attributes. Praise God for who He is. Thank Him for what He does. Praise God for His matchless attributes. Begin all your prayers with praise. Your life will never be the same. When you understand who God is, your attitude about life changes.

What can we learn about the boy in this story: The Greatest Hitter in the World?
A little boy was standing alone with a baseball repeating, "I am the greatest hitter in the world."
He then threw up the ball, swung, and missed. "Strike one!" He said.
Then he said again, "I am the greatest hitter in the world."
He threw the ball up, swung again, and missed again. "Strike two!"
He said. "I am the greatest hitter in the world."
The third time he swung, he missed again, "Strike three!"
He thought for a moment and shouted, "I am the greatest pitcher in the world!"

Watch Gideon's transformation of trust. How did Gideon do against the Midianites he feared so much? How did he overcome his deepest fears?
Judges 7:1-25

There is nothing that you and God can't do together.
- What wine press has you caged?
- What is holding you back from trusting God with abandon?
- Where do you need to step over the wine press?
- What fear is holding you from being God's mighty warrior?

Break into groups of three or four.

Where has fear separated how God sees you and how you see yourself?

Take a moment today and pray for each other.

STUDY NOTES

_____

_____

_____

_____

_____

_____

_____

_____

_____

_____

_____

_____

_____

For the next five days, read the following entries from our **The Field Guide: A Bathroom Book for Men.**

We hope they challenge and encourage you to get in the great Arena for God. See you on the Arena Floor!

SOUL POWER

The Sovereign Lord is my strength; he makes my feet like the feet of a deer, he enables me to go on the heights.
~ Habakkuk 3:19

The gestation period of humans is a long time at nearly nine months. Babies take years to wean, walk, and talk—let alone survive on their own. Comparably, we are slow and weak. We're practically hairless. We have no teeth or claws to rip and kill. Our scent is so rancid a predator can locate us from miles away. Left alone, we'd be extinct in a couple of generations, if not a couple of hours.

Practically speaking we are woefully and pathetically made. But the Bible says, "I praise you because I am fearfully and wonderfully made" (Psalm 139:14).

Still, man remains the greatest predator on the planet.

We are created in God's image. God has given us an imprint by which to have dominion over creation—a living soul (Genesis 1:26-28). The human mind is far superior to other animals. We can overcome our physical limitations with the mental capacity that has put a man on the moon and beyond.

God has placed a holy terror among the animal kingdom in the form of mankind. God has given us unique abilities to dominate creation in spite of our physical limitations.

But it's an outside source that determines man's strength. It's that Source that deserves our worship. That, of course, is God. Looking at humans as a species how could anyone ever believe in anything but God?

Unfortunately, men are stubborn and choose to worship lesser, created gods. But strength comes when a man acknowledges that the "Sovereign Lord is my strength."

UNSCHOOLED

When they saw the courage of Peter and John and realized that they were unschooled, ordinary men,
they were astonished and they took note that these men had been with Jesus.
~ Acts 4:13

Years ago, a man responded to my faith story with: "My mom was very sick when she was pregnant with me and I was supposed to be born handicapped or worse, but through the prayers of godly grandparents I am healthy and normal. I know I'm a miracle. I agree with you about Jesus, but I don't want to stop living my life."

He was afraid that following Jesus would make him less of a man. Sadly, his view of Christianity was skewed—or should I say screwed—by the effeminate influences in so many churches today. What this man failed to recognize is that he's a shell of the miracle God created him to be.

He is less of a man without Jesus.

His church experiences clouded the fact that trusting God could make him more of a man, not less. A man will never reach his full potential by living apart from the God who made him. It's impossible. His capacity for life can only be achieved by radical devotion to Jesus.

You may disagree. You're still wrong. Get over yourself.

Today's verse proves what God can do through men who ruthlessly trust him. God turns males into men. God makes ordinary men extraordinary.

What's the naked truth about faith?

It's so simple. I hate repeating it but we're often stubborn aren't we? The answer to becoming a man is found in Matthew 6:33: "But seek first His kingdom and His righteousness, and all these things will be given to you as well."

Ordinary men become extraordinary when they ruthlessly trust in their God.

COURAGE MELTED

They mounted up to the heavens and went down to the depths; in their peril their courage melted away.
~ Psalm 107:26

I was reminded of the power of God while on a fishing trip in Sitka, Alaska with my Dad and brother. Dad has battled seasickness his entire life. He survived the first two days of our trip, but the waves grew rougher and on the third day Dad almost fell overboard while losing his breakfast over the back of the boat.

Those waves were a small gesture of God's capability.

Think about how mighty God is in nature. The bravest of men will run for cover in the path of a tornado. The strongest of men will run from the leaping flames of a wildfire. The smartest of men will be silenced in awe of the galaxies.

The most athletic of men will concede to the depths of God's great oceans. The most ingenious of men will surrender to gravitational pull falling from 30,000 feet in the air.

Our perspective of God changes when we compare the power of God to our minuscule speck in creation. We are so small. I think the late Rich Mullins said it best, "We are not as strong as we think we are."

We cower in fear, melt away in despair, and shudder in panic, when faced with the reality of God.

Courage, even in the bravest men, will be "melted away" when standing before the Creator of the universe.

In fact, no man will stand.

Every knee will bow (Philippians 2:9-10). This is a legitimate fear. It's the kind that melts human courage in the face of the Divine. True courage, then, comes to the man who has been melted by the presence of God.

MARCHING ORDERS

"Come here and put your feet on the necks of these kings." So they came forward and placed their feet on their necks. Joshua said to them, "Do not be afraid; do not be discouraged. Be strong and courageous. This is what the Lord will do to all the enemies you are going to fight." Then Joshua struck and killed the kings and hung them on five trees, and they were left hanging on the trees until evening.
~ Joshua 10:24-26

Today's passage arrives at one of the most epic battles in Biblical history. Joshua's army has defeated the stronger alliance of the kings of Jerusalem, Hebron, Jarmuth, Lachish, and Eglon (Joshua 10:5).

Imagine being one of Joshua's soldiers with your foot pressed firmly into the neck of the king of Jerusalem. The blood of your enemies is still sticky on your hands. You can feel the warmth of the sun standing still in the sky. You're exhausted from an all-night march and all-day battle (9). During the day, baseball sized hailstones killed thousands of the enemy—but none of you (11).

The sun refused to set and the moon didn't rise until the battle was won
~ Joshua 10:13

How, Who, What could have caused these miraculous events? With your foot pressed into the neck of a wide-eyed king, you realize something—God is real. He is who He says He is. You can trust Him. The king you feared is under your foot. His head will soon be removed from his body. No king or obstacle is too big for God to defeat.

The question today is this: Who will you fear?

It's a question every man must answer. Joshua trusted in God and he marched all night to victory. Joshua's faith caused him to march headlong into battle and victory. Trust God.

Start marching.

SNAGGED

When Ish-Bosheth son of Saul heard that Abner had died in Hebron, he lost courage, and all Israel became alarmed.
~ 2 Samuel 4:1

You can imagine how many lures I lost as a child learning how to cast; often snagging them on trees, rocks, or forgetting to take my finger off the spool. I learned one of three things is to blame for a lost lure: the fish, the line, or the fisherman.

Growing up I lost far more lures than I caught fish. I got pretty good at blaming the fish while holding a frayed line dangling aimlessly in the wind, and Dad muttering obscenities under his breath —sometimes screaming them!

Today's passage reveals a man who got snagged casting his courage to another man. Courage can't be deferred, but followers often hide behind their leader's courage. This is only a Band-Aid. Every man, no matter how good, eventually disappoints. Even the greatest men have flaws. Courage cast in the wrong direction will eventually snag.

The great warrior Abner eventually died, but Ish-Bosheth mistakenly cast his trust upon him rather than God. He learned the hard way that no man can carry the burden for him. Maybe that's why Peter (speaking about Jesus) implored, "Cast all your anxiety on him because he cares for you" (1 Peter 5:7).

Like the hundreds of lures snagged (and lost) over the years, casting courage in the wrong direction ultimately breaks. No man is worthy of your courage.

The phrase "lost courage" in today's passage literally means "his hands dropped." In other words, he made a bad cast. His shoulders slumped in defeat. His head hung low. His spirit was broken.

Trust in what will never fray or snap under resistance. Discover the power that comes from casting our courage upon the One who will never fail. The man who trusts in Him will not get snagged.

TEAM MEETING TEN:
FORGED BY GOD

What did you take away from last week's study and daily readings? What are you still processing? What challenged your current paradigm? What inspired you to grow as a man?

Have you ever experienced the discipline of God? What is it about being forged by God that makes us so averse to it?
Proverbs 3:11-13, Romans 5:3-5, and Hebrews 12:1-7

"In ancient times a warrior did not go down to a sporting goods store and buy broadheads. He would start with some type of rock or volcanic glass that could be knapped into a sharp point. The tip of an arrow or spear would be cultivated over hours, if not days to get the correct point, sharpness, and shape.
The time spent cultivating this weapon assured the warrior that at the given time he would be able to utilize the fruits of his labor to either protect his family, or to provide nourishment to those he loved. If the warrior neglected to shape the spearhead he would be left with just a rock. But by knapping away all of the excess rock he would be able to focus all his power to a single point."
~ Chad Azevedo, Men In The Arena Board Member

TEAM MEETING AT A GLANCE

- Opening Prayer, Weekly Announcements
- Personal and Victory Stories
- Each man will share his story — one man per week until all men have shared.
- After all men have shared their personal story, allow time each week for them to share victory stories.
- Weekly Study Closing Prayer
- Closing Prayer

> *"No pain, no gain."*
> ~ Poster

Who is the last person to chip away at your dullness? When was the last time you were hammered by God?
Proverbs 27:17

Forge Defined: "To make or shape (a metal object) by heating it in a fire or furnace and beating or hammering it." Google Search

Before steel is forged it must be refined. How does God refine us? Who does God use to refine you? What role does a good wife play in forging us?
Psalm 66:10, Isaiah 48:10, and Daniel 12:10

Break up into groups of two or three max. Search out times in the gospels (Matthew, Mark, Luke, and John) when you see Jesus forging his men.

What opportunities does Jesus use to forge The Disciples? How does this translate to your life?

The origin of forging may be traced to the ancient process of hammering of gold between a rock (the anvil), and a stone (the hammer). In hammering, the inertia of the fast-moving hammer provides the required deformation energy and force, while in pressing the force is static.

> *"You cannot dream yourself into a character: you must hammer and forge yourself into one."*
> ~ Henry David Thoreau

Usually the final shape is imparted on the workpiece by manipulating the workpiece between the flat anvil and the flat hammer as the hammer hits the workpiece repeatedly. A conical protrusion from the anvil, holes in the anvil, a variety of pegs with different cross sections, and auxiliary tools, including a large selection of shaped hand hammers, may assist the blacksmiths and their helpers.
~ www.metalforming-inc.com

How does God use pain and suffering to hammer us into the men He requires? So many quit when they face pain. Endure it. Persevere in pain until you find resolution. How can you take it like a man?
1 Peter 1:6-8, Romans 5:2-4, 8:16-18, Philippians 3:9-11, Colossians 1:24, and 2 Timothy 2:2-4

How is forging similar to pruning? What is God cutting out of your life? What needs to be cut?
John 15:1-3

How are they different?

What do you think of God's promise of persecution? How does God use persecution to forge something stronger in us?
Matthew 5:9-12, John 15:19-21, 1 Corinthians 4:11-13, and 2 Timothy 3:10-13

> *"Leadership is getting someone to do what they don't want to do,*
> *to achieve what they want to achieve."*
> ~ Tom Landry

Stay in your groups of two and three.

Share a godly characteristic you'd like God to forge in you.

Take a moment today and pray for each other.

STUDY NOTES

_____

_____

_____

_____

_____

_____

_____

_____

_____

_____

_____

_____

For the next five days, read the following entries from our **The Field Guide: A Bathroom Book for Men.**

We hope they challenge and encourage you to get in the great Arena for God. See you on the Arena Floor!

STOUTHEARTED

When I called, you answered me; you made me bold and stouthearted.
~ Psalms 138:3

We're living in the technological Renaissance. It's a world of instant information with many forms of communication. It's a world that defines a friend as someone whose picture you accepted into your social media world.

The personal phone call has become a means to test my friendship status. I've discovered that friends answer most of my calls while acquaintances tend to send me to voicemail.

Thankfully, God doesn't live in that world. He answers every time. He may not tell me what I want to hear but He will answer every time. The personal touch changes things.

A personal relationship with Christ changes everything.

A relationship with God compelled stuttering Moses to stand against Pharaoh. A relationship with God caused Gideon to step out of the wine press and lay hold of his mighty warrior. A relationship with God caused Abraham to "Go to the land I will show you" (Genesis 12:1).

A relationship with God caused Paul to lean on Christ's strength with his thorn in his flesh. A relationship with God caused Peter to preach to the multitudes after denying Christ.

A relationship with God turns weakness into boldness. God makes a man more of a man than he ever dreamed without Him.

I love the New American Standard's translation of today's passage:
"You made me bold with strength in my soul."

A man is better with Christ than without Him. When Christ comes into a man, the man comes alive (2 Corinthians 5:17).

Call on God today. He'll answer every time.

GATHER IT

Joseph of Arimathea, a prominent member of the Council, who was himself waiting for the kingdom of God, went boldly to Pilate and asked for Jesus' body.
~ Mark 15:43

On June 1, 2012, my family and I became full-time crusaders for men through our fledgling organization called The Great Hunt for God. We knew God would do mighty things, but the idea of raising thousands of dollars a month from donors was nearly paralyzing.

I can almost understand the fear Joseph of Arimathea may have felt when he "went boldly to Pilate and asked for Jesus' body."

Our first year was a faith journey as God walked me through a debilitating back injury, failed surgery, tragedy of some dear friends, the suicide of my step-father, our house going into foreclosure, and sending our oldest son away to college.

The New American Standard translation of Mark 15:43 says, "and he gathered up courage and went before Pilate." Can you imagine Joseph gathering his courage? What did that look like?

Maybe Joseph went to his friends for prayer and words of encouragement. Maybe he had Peter urge him on. Maybe he prayed. He did everything he could to muster the courage to ask for Jesus' body. When he'd gathered all the courage he could, he went to Pilate.

Looking back, 2012 was the most difficult year of my life. But The Great Hunt did more than simply survive. It gained momentum. By the end of that year we had an organizational contingency fund, published two books, preached the gospel in six states, trained missionaries in a foreign country, launched fourteen teams across three states, and received commitments to launch The Great Hunt for God from several others. All of that with a back injury that only allowed twenty hours of work per week.

How does that happen? God.

When we surrender to the power of God, we set our fear aside and gather courage.

WYOMING NIGHTS

...in order that I may boast on the day of Christ that I did not run or labor for nothing.
~ Philippians 2:16

While camping in Wyoming's Grizzly country with some hunting buddies, we were awakened by a strange creature pushing against our tent. The creature's grunts and snorts created a hushed discussion about what to do next. The man closest to the door (fortunately not me) slowly unzipped the tent, preparing for attack.

The zipper's sound erupted the silence.

Even the crickets held their breath. The tent door opened to reveal the horrifying brown silhouette of one of our untied horses! I thought for sure that we'd be eaten alive by an angry Grizzly, though I never admitted it. We laughed it off hoping no one else heard the pounding of our hearts.

Men struggle to admit their deepest fears.

More than being ripped to shreds by a man-eating Grizzly, my greatest fear is of wasting my life. I don't want to die until I've accomplished what God wants from me.

My soul longs to hear Jesus say, "Well done, good and faithful servant"
(Matthew 25: 23).

How tragic it would be for a man to reach the end of his climb only to discover that he submitted the wrong mountain.

The only thing worse would be to finish in the fields of faith, only to stand before the God who gave everything for me and realize I didn't leave it all on the field for Him.

Consider the day when you see the Master face to face. That day will come sooner than you think. What will He say to you? How will you respond? Live to respond with Luke 17:10 on your lips, "We are unworthy servants; we have only done our duty."

THE GUIDE

May the Lord direct your hearts into God's love and Christ's perseverance.
~ 2 Thessalonians 3:5

Amos said he had directions to a hot fishing spot in Idaho's Red Mountains, but I should've taken more notice when he admitted to never actually fishing there. We made the two-hour drive to the trailhead, hiked six miles to a pristine mountain lake and began casting. Large trout were jumping everywhere, but three hours later we caught nothing.

Discouraged, we followed the trail home but after a mile or so I noticed Amos made a right turn at a fork where he should have gone left. He's the guide. Maybe he knows something I don't, I reasoned. So, I followed him blindly.

Three miles later he stopped dead in his tracks, put his head down, and turned, and faced me, "I have to confess something. I have no idea where we are."

I told him about the fork in the trail, got in front, and led us back to the intersection. A few hours later we navigated our way out of the mountains— tired and dehydrated—but alive.

In today's passage Paul prays, "The Lord direct your hearts into God's love and Christ's perseverance." Jesus stands at the crossroads of God's love. But it doesn't stop there. Salvation is just the beginning of the story.

The trail forks where perseverance begins. Faith must persevere beyond the moment of salvation or what's the point. The journey to God is an upward climb. Ignore anyone who tells you different. This is not an easy journey.

But it's well worth it.

Jesus never told his followers to make decisions (an event), but make disciples (a process). How many followers of Jesus walk in defeat, wandering aimlessly through life as if lost though they are found? They've neglected the process of salvation.

FIRST THINGS FIRST

Yet I hold this against you: You have forsaken your first love. Remember the height from which you have fallen! Repent and do the things you did at first. If you do not repent, I will come to you and remove your lamp stand from its place.
~ Revelation 2:4-5

During my days as Youth for Christ Director, a co-worker gave me a tent that he couldn't get rid of at his garage sale. Excited at his zealous generosity, I gladly accepted. As soon as the tent was in my hands he said, "Hey, can I have your water ski?" Realizing his motives were more about the ski than the tent, I offered it back.

His generosity was right, but for the wrong reasons. How often have you caught yourself doing the right thing, but for the wrong reason? Your outside didn't match the inside.

The church at Ephesus had similar issues. They'd become experts at sniffing out lies, doing good works, and persevering. They looked great on paper, but a deeper issue lurked under the surface.

They'd lost their passion for Jesus.

They'd stopped doing the things they did when nothing mattered but Jesus. They became experts in doing the right things. But they neglected the most important thing.

They were committed to the marriage, but rejected the romance. They played the game but forgot the love.

Who was Revelation 2:4-5 addressed to? Was it to a group of people or an individual? The indictment was directed to the overseers responsible for caring for the church—the pastors. It was a warning to spiritual leaders. The spiritual leader's priority for those he leads is Jesus.

Jesus is, and must always be, the first. He is what matters most. When a man gets this—everyone wins.

NOW WHAT?!?

You just finished Book 1 of the Strong Men Study Series, defining the five essentials of manhood. You may be wondering, "Now what do I do?"

Thanks for asking. You have three options.
Option Uno: You can look for other resources for the men on your team.

Nah, we're just kidding. That's not an option.
Option Dos: You can move on to one of the other five books in the Strong Men Study Series until you've completed all five books, fifty of the team meetings, and 250 daily readings.

Those books are:

Book 1: The Trailhead: Protecting Integrity

Book 2: The Climb: Fighting Apathy

Book 3: The Summit: Pursuing God Passionately

Book 4: The Descent: Leading Courageously

Book 5: Trail's End: Finishing Strong

Option Tres: Visit our website (www.meninthearena.org) for other great resources to guide you to your best version of a man.

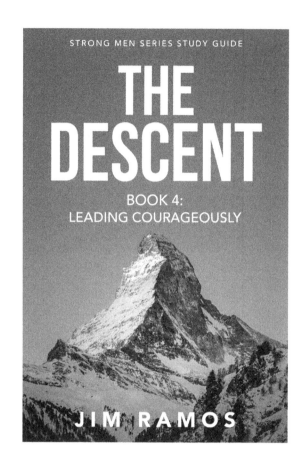

THE BATHROOM BOOK

Men are confused about what a man is. Is he a hunter, an extreme sports guy, or religious? Is he strong, a warrior, or a fighter? Is he a great athlete, rich, or famous?

Better yet, how does a male know when he's crossed into manhood? Is it chronological age? Is it anatomical? Is it when he is legally called a man? Is it becoming financially independent?

Where does a man learn about being a man? Is it from his dad, a coach, television, Google, The Bachelor, or possibly Chuck Norris?

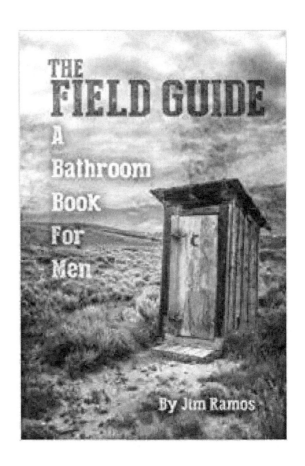

In the Field Guide: A Bathroom Book for Men, Jim Ramos uses his unique storytelling ability to tie masculine words in Scripture with everyday life. Day after inspiring day, the Field Guide weaves biblical themes of masculinity throughout the five essentials of manhood, "protecting integrity, fighting apathy, pursuing God passionately, leading courageously and finishing strong."

This book is a must-read for men. Place it at your bedside, in your office, man cave, or the back of your toilet. Use it as your favorite bathroom book. Read it daily. But be careful. The paper is no substitute for the real deal and will cut you! Only use it for reading!

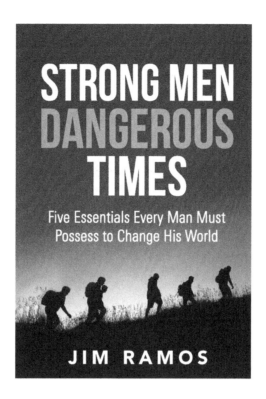

STRONG MEN DANGEROUS TIMES

Weldon M. Hardenbrook wrote, "Let's face it. It's extremely difficult for men to act like men when so much confusion exists about the definition of manhood. For most of human history, people knew what it meant to be a man. Now, at least in modern America, no one seems to know."

But men are conquerors. They seek the next hill to die on. They long for a mission to accomplish. They need a target to shoot at, but the sights have become blurry. Men are staring aimlessly through a dense fog of cultural ambiguity, and those they love are paying the price.

In his book Strong Men Dangerous Times: Five Essentials Every Man Must Possess to Change His World, Jim Ramos answers the question men have been asking for years, "What is a man?"

The simplicity of the book is brilliantly designed for the man who's too busy to read. It's short, to the point, and loaded with life application stories and will keep you on the edge of your seat!

Order your copy today.

ENLIST IN OUR ARMY

Facebook Forum

Join thousands of men from around the world in an open discussion on manhood! The Men in the Arena is a closed group for men only. It is the best free resource for men to discuss what a man is and does. Get out of the anonymous bleachers and into the Arena today!

Weekly Equipping Blast

Visit our website and subscribe to our weekly Equipping Blast. This is not spam or advertising. It is our weekly effort to guide you towards your best version.

Podcast

Subscribe to the Men in the Arena Podcast and learn from the top authors and experts on manhood on the planet.

GLOSSARY

The Definition (aka Five Essentials or Man Card): The Men in the Arena definition of manhood is "protecting integrity, fighting apathy, pursuing God passionately, leading courageously, and finishing strong." These are the things a man does to keep his Man Card.

Dioko: The Greek word the Apostle Paul used in Philippians 3:12 and 14 for "press on" meaning to hunt, pursue, or chase. It's where our name for The Great Hunt for God originated before we changed it to Men in the Arena!

Equipping Blast: Our weekly email blast is sent to thousands of men around the world. It includes our blog, podcast links, training videos, and more! Sign up at meninthearena.org.

Fighting Apathy: The second of the five characteristics of manhood demanding that men fight against all cultural resistance threatening to pull them down. Failure to resist this friction over time becomes apathy or callousness. Matthew 13:13-15 defines "callousness" as a lack of feeling that results when we fail to fight against the things trying to push us down. The second book in the Strong Men Study Series: The Climb, is dedicated to this topic.

Financial Champion: Did you know Men in the Arena is a crowd-funded organization? Crowd-funded means we strategically partner with generous people like you to fund our ministry. Please consider joining our great team of financial champions by signing up as a monthly donor on our website.

Finishing Strong: This is the last of the five traits of manhood, imploring men to finish every day strong to finish life strong. Each day's strong finish compounded over time completes a strong life finish.

Finishing is not the same as finishing strong. Please refer to 2 Timothy 4:6-7. The fifth book in the Strong Men Study Series: The Trail's End is dedicated to this topic.

Guardrails: Imagine traveling on the narrow road Jesus spoke of in Matthew 7:13-14. Its borders are lined with guardrails meant to direct and protect you as you travel through life. Guardrails are walls or hedges a man builds around himself and those he loves. Deuteronomy 22:8 is a great reference for building guardrails.

Intergenerational: One of the core values of the Men in the Arena is to lock shields with men representing all generations and decades of life.

Leading Courageously: The fourth of five aspects of The Definition imploring a man to step up and assume the role as patriarch and spiritual leader of the household. The fourth book in the Strong Men Study Series: The Descent, is dedicated to this topic.

Protecting Integrity: The first and foundational component in the Man Card describing the man who is mature, complete, and unbroken. Integrity is the sum of all character traits fully formed in a man. The first book in the Strong Men Study Series: The Trailhead, is dedicated to this topic.

Pursuing God Passionately: The third and climactic component of the Man Card. It's our adamant belief that no man can achieve his original design without radical obedience and relentless pursuit of his Creator and King. The third book in the Strong Men Study Series: The Summit, is dedicated to this topic.

Tag Line: We say it all the time. "When a man gets it - everyone wins!!"

Team Meeting: The weekly gathering of the Men in the Arena. Team meetings are designed to be no more than one hour in length and set to meet at the same time and place each week at the discretion of the team captains.

Vision: Our vision is simply trusting Jesus Christ to build an army of Men in the Arena, who are becoming their best version in Christ, and changing their world (because when a man gets it - everyone wins!).

COACHING TIPS

This Coaching Tips section is designed to help both new and seasoned Team Captains.

It offers helpful hints we've discovered in our years of running small groups with men.

Our one request is that you don't veer off course and go rogue with your team meetings. Our coaching tips are tried and true.

Feel free to add your personal style but avoid making it up as you go. We've been there—done that— and want to spare you the humiliation! Good hunting.

Big brother is watching: Your guys are watching you. They're watching how you live, love, serve, and run all team meetings.
Be an example.

Bring your A-Game: Bring your A-Game to the team meetings. Know who will and will not be present. Come prepared with notes in your workbook. If you have a co-captain, make sure you're on the same page. Men know when you come unprepared. This sends the wrong message.

Dynamics: How your team members are positioned in the room is crucial. The men need to sit at eye level and equidistant from the center of an eight-foot (maximum) diameter circle. If your circle, or any man, is further than four feet from center, your discussions will be greatly hindered.

Finger on the pulse: Your team will take on a unique identity. The morale of the men is at different levels, and group dynamics change constantly. What is the heartbeat of your men? Who's been missing? Who seems disengaged? Are you connecting with your co-captain(s)? What does your team need this week?

Floor Stare: Try this the next time you ask a question. Stare at the floor or at your workbook until guys begin to answer. Let them deal with the awkward silence and figure out an answer on their own.

Half Full Glass: Transforming lives is a journey. It's an investment into the lives of imperfect men. Even though these books are broken into ten-week bricks, our goal is to make a long-term investment in the transformational process.

But life is tough, and people are messy. When you lead your team, make sure to be positive. The negative will be easier to spot but be careful to acknowledge more positive than negative. It will pay dividends in the end.

Preparation is Key: Come prepared and ready to lead your team each week. The men on your team are watching you. They see the scribbled pages of preparation within the margins of The Man Card Series pages.

They also notice the blank pages when you come unprepared. Don't wing it and fling it. Bring your own thoughts and ideas to the table at every team meeting.

NEW TEAM LAUNCH STEPS

The Launch Steps are a tool to help Captains start a successful team.

Launch Step One: Co-Captain

Although it is not mandatory that you do this to launch a team, we highly recommend that you have another man to lock shields with through this process. There will be times you can't make it to the group, and it's good to know that someone has your back.

Besides recruiting team members, leaders often confess that finding their co-captain was the most challenging step in launching a new team. If you already have your co-captain, great job!

If you're struggling to find a co-captain, don't be discouraged. It's normal! When you approach a potential co-captain, and he has questions about the Men in the Arena and what you're asking him to do, send him to our website (www.meninthearena.org).

There, he can join our online forum, subscribe to our Equipping Blast, and receive all the information about Men in the Arena he needs to feel confident. Now you're ready to take on Launch Step Two.

Launch Step Two: Hit List

Hopefully, you were able to recruit a co-captain. If so, congratulations! Now it's time to put together your team. That's what building the Hit List is all about. Did you know that Jesus recruited a larger group of disciples before he chose the Twelve? Check it out:

"One of those days, Jesus went out to a mountainside to pray, and spent the night praying to God. When morning came, he called his disciples to him and chose twelve of them, whom he also designated apostles: Simon (whom he named Peter), his brother Andrew, James, John, Philip, Bartholomew, Matthew, Thomas, James, son of Alphaeus, Simon who was called the Zealot, Judas, son of James, and Judas Iscariot, who became a traitor."
Luke 6:12-16

With your co-captain, create two Hit Lists of at least 10-15 potential recruits—yours and his. Commit your Hit List to prayer, asking God to direct you through the process.

Once both lists have been compiled, pray over them, and decide who will receive a formal "call" (Launch Step Three) to be on your team. Some Team Captains invite all the men on their Hit Lists, while others are more selective. This is personal preference. Some Captains struggle to recruit enough men for their team. Others have to cut their Hit List down. Team size should range from a minimum of six to fourteen members maximum.

If possible, create an intergenerational team of men ranging throughout multiple decades of life. Once the Hit List is created, move on to Launch Step Three.

Launch Step Three: Call

Before you call each man, make sure you have the set time, date, and place of your first meeting—the Team Launch. This is important: you and your co-captain set the meeting day, time, and place, then tell the men. Don't ask the men what they prefer.

Make a decision before inviting men to join your team. Captains that try to please everyone on this issue lose. Some men won't be able to join your team simply because of your meeting times. That's normal, and you must be okay with it.

Once verbal commitments are made, move on to Launch Step Four.

Launch Step Four: Team List

How Captains communicate with their teams is partly what separates the good teams from the great ones. The Team List will be used on the Buy-In (Launch Step Six) and must include: Name (and wife's name), e-mail (and wife's e-mail), and cell phone number. The sooner an e-mail and text group are created, the more effective your team will be.

Use the Team List to remind the men about your weekly meetings. This acts as a reminder and gives men a simple way to reply if they can't make it that week.

We recommend putting together a calendar of key events for your team. Include your launch day, time, and place of weekly meeting, Team Potluck (Launch Step Five), and other important dates such as birthdays, important anniversaries, and regular social gatherings.

Launch Step Five: Team Potluck

You're almost there! You only have a few more steps until your Team Launch! Great job! We can't overemphasize the importance of the Team Potluck, especially for the married men. Use your Team List to communicate the time, date, and location of the Team Potluck.

Give your potential team at least three weeks' notice to save the date and communicate with their wives (Who should also be included in the email). We have found that the wives are usually the ones who manage the family calendar.

You should also invite the pastor who oversees small groups at your church. Have him pray for the meal and say a few words about the value of men in God's agenda.

Your goal is 100% attendance of those invited. One Team Captain confessed that he opted out of the potluck to hurry the process, and it was a monumental mistake.

The goal of the Team Potluck is to get total buy-in from the wives and have all questions answered. If the wife is in, the man is in. Trust us! We've seen it over and over. Attendance by the wives is critical for the success of Team Potluck.

Team Potluck Sample Agenda
- Dinner Responsibilities
- Captains supply the drinks and dessert
- Host home supplies dinnerware
- A-M Main Dish
- N-Z Salad (or dessert)

Sample Agenda (make it better)
- Fellowship
- Food (remember to pray before eating!)
- Captain and wife introductions
- Team member and wife introductions
- Review Team Launch information (day, time, and place), commitment level (75% attendance), and other pertinent information
- Explain the Buy-In (Launch Step Six)
- Q and A
- Pray for the group

Team Captain Commission: We believe in partnership with the local church and highly encourage Team Captains to get commissioned by a pastor or spiritual leader. If at all possible, get commissioned during the worship service at the church you attend. If not, the potluck is an appropriate option.

Fellowship

Launch Step Six: Buy-In

You can almost taste your Team Launch at his point. We're as excited as you to see lives transformed through your team!

All that's left is to order the books. Attrition will most likely claim some of the men, but we have found that the more the men buy in, the more committed they will be.

You can either buy the resources yourself, and the men reimburse you or send them directly to www.meninthearena.org and purchase the curriculum themselves.

Launch Step Seven: Commission and Launch

We hinted at this in launch Step Five: Team Potluck. Did you know that in the New Testament, the Twelve Apostles, the Apostle Paul—and Jesus—were commissioned in ministry? Have you been commissioned?

If not, we highly recommend it as a model for spiritual leadership. We believe so much in the local church that we strongly urge all team captains to be commissioned by their pastor or spiritual leader. Make it a public display. Here are some elements of a commission.

- Ceremony or public worship service
- Anointing and/or laying on of hands
- Public words of affirmation
- Giving of gifts (optional)
- Witnesses
- Spiritual leader
- Predecessor
- The Holy Spirit

Launch Step Eight: Team Launch Meeting One

Today's the day you've been working so hard for—Congratulations! This is an informational meeting only. Do not plan on going through the curriculum. Rather, make sure all of the men have it. If you don't meet where food and drinks are served, make sure they are available. Your first meeting should be one hour long from your designated start time (start on time, end on time).

Below is a sample agenda.

- Fellowship over food and drinks (10 minutes)
- Opening Prayer
- Restate the purpose, expectations, meeting agenda. Make sure they have purchased their books. (5 minutes)
- Men share about their lives, what they expect to get from the group, and where they are in their spiritual journey (40 minutes)
- Encourage and inspire them with your personal vision for the team. Be sensitive to where each man is. Be careful not to push too hard too fast. (5 minutes)
- Closing Prayer

Thank you so much for getting out of the anonymous bleachers and into the Arena! We are pumped to partner with you on your new adventure!

ABOUT JIM RAMOS

Thank you for taking your precious time to work through this book. I am honored and hope it inspired you on your journey towards the best you.

Lets lock arms on our journey. You can follow my journey on Facebook, Twitter, or Instagram @jimwramos.

I've been married to my best friend Shanna since 1992. She's the most important person in my life and my best friend. We love drinking coffee, traveling to tropical places, and eating out with friends.

I'm an avid book reader, enjoy fitness in the great outdoors, but my real passion is hunting. My sons are my hunting partners, along with a select few guys.

I love hanging out with men over a cup of good coffee and learning their stories. You can learn more about my story at meninthearena.org

Made in the USA
Las Vegas, NV
25 September 2021